Sexism in Children's Books
Facts, figures & guidelines

Papers on Children's Literature No.2 edited by the Children's Rights Workshop

A collection of introductory articles on sexism in children's literature

Writers and Readers Publishing Cooperative

Introduction © Children's Rights Workshop
Sex-Role Socialization © American Journal of Sociology
Sexism in Award Winning Picture Books © Suzanne M Czaplinski
Sex-Roles in Reading Schemes © Forum
McGraw-Hill Guidelines © McGraw-Hill Book Company

Published 1976 by Writers and Readers Publishing Cooperative
14 Talacre Road, London NW5 3PE

Illustrations by Lee Robinson

Contents

Introduction
page 1

Sex-Role Socialization in Picture Books for Preschool Children
page 5

Sexism in Award Winning Picture Books
page 31

Sex-Roles in Reading Schemes
page 38

The McGraw-Hill Guidelines
page 45

Acknowledgements

We should like to thank Ms. Lenore Weitzman, Ms. Suzanne Czaplinski, Ms. Glenys Lobban and the McGraw-Hill Book Company for their kind permission to reproduce the articles in this pamphlet. Ms. Weitzman et al's article first appeared in the *American Journal of Sociology* Vol 77, no.6 May 1972. The complete version of Ms. Czaplinski's article is available from Know Inc., P.O. Box 86031, Pittsburgh, Penn. 15221, USA ($2.00). Ms. Lobban's article first appeared in *Forum*, Spring 1974, Vol 16, no.2. The McGraw-Hill Guidelines may be reproduced in whole or in part without written permission provided that each such reproduction carries an acknowledgement to the McGraw-Hill Book Company.

Introduction
Children's Rights Workshop

Sexism (via Racism) and McGraw-Hill

It is of the nature of the communications industry in British society that, while sexism is still a fairly unfamiliar concept today, references to 'Women's Lib' rarely leave the headlines. On the other hand, the force of the social and political demands of the women's movement in many countries is such that the struggle against women's exploitation and oppression — against sexism — now constitutes one of the most dynamic and conscious movements in the world today. If the fight against sexism is fundamental to the international women's movement, the word sexism itself grew out of an analogy with racism, itself now a universally familiar concept and the subject of perhaps the most dynamic and conscious of world movements today, i.e. the struggle of non-white, non-Western peoples for economic and political autonomy, cultural freedom and the right to self-determination.

Sexism then can generally be used to denote discrimination based on gender. This definition is taken from the McGraw-Hill Guidelines, reprinted here, which appeared in May 1974 'to eliminate sexist assumptions from McGraw-Hill Book Company publications'. These Guidelines provide a precise and useful weapon against sexism in children's books and other literature and are particularly significant in that they see sexism as applying to men as well as women. As the Guidelines themselves point out, sexism at one stage 'only referred to prejudice against the female sex'. In the words of another US book firm's *Guidelines for Improving the Image of Women in Textbooks* (Scott Foresman) 'sexism refers to all those attitudes and actions which relegate women to secondary and inferior status in society'. The Scott Foresman Guidelines, published in 1972, reflect an early but still current understanding of sexism, namely that it only applies to women. In 1974 when the McGraw-Hill Guidelines were stressing that males and females were equally stereotyped in literature, the Scott Foresman definition was still circulating, for example as part of the 'Non-Sexist Curricular Materials for Elementary Schools' by Laurie Olsen Johnson (Feminist Press).

These conflicting definitions are indicative of a many-faceted and yet developing awareness which has stimulated a mass of Guidelines*, checklists, criteria, recommendations, all geared to eradicate sexism in all its forms. The McGraw-Hill Guidelines stand out as the best example of such campaigning material and provide in our opinion the most relevant definition of sexism.

One of the purposes of these 'Papers . . .' is to inform a wider public of the value of the concept of sexism as a means to understanding and as a critical tool, particularly in relation to children's literature. As this pamphlet hopefully shows, sexism in literature is expressed in the use of vocabulary and in the presentation of people, roles and situations. For those new to the concept or unsure of its relevance to their lives or work, the McGraw-Hill Guidelines are a particularly good introduction to sexism in vocabulary and everyday speech. The awareness of sexist assumptions in language is now widely recognised as an important step in the fight against sex-discrimination. Although issued by a US publishing house for the attention of its staff, the McGraw-Hill Guidelines can be usefully applied in this country and to most situations, in report and letter writing, in public speeches as well as in private if not intimate conversations. Language is central to the speech, thinking and culture of any society. To tackle the assumptions behind language, by using alternative words and thus exploring alternative concepts, is the challenge of the McGraw-Hill Guidelines.

Old Problems: New Strategies

Although the Guidelines cover a much wider field than children's literature and are concerned in fact with all literature, the rest of the items reprinted in this pamphlet are purely concerned with children's books, and picture books in particular. They are reproduced here as the best elements known to us that together introduce the question of sexism in children's books. Alongside the examples given in the Guidelines, the arguments and statistical evidence of the other items should provide conclusive proof not only that sexism has flourished in children's literature for many years but also that it continues to do so despite important changes in attitudes and in society generally. (See Czaplinski extracts.)

If the overall message of these 'Papers . . .' is a gloomy one that suggests that there is a lot to be done, it is not that no efforts are being made by publishers (a few), librarians and teachers (some) to introduce to children a literature that reflects realities that they can recognise and build on. But most effort seems to be directed at the importing and translation of children's literature from the more socially progressive countries (e.g. Denmark, Sweden), rather than directed at the understanding of the processes of sexism in children's books, at recognising its manifestations in our literature and at encouraging non-biased writing and illustration by British writers and artists.

* Published in April 1976 is the first British 'Guidelines': *Non-Sexist Code of Practice for Book Publishing.* Available from Women in Publishing Industry c/o 19 Novello St., London SW6. Send 10p and an s.a.e.

It is to be hoped that publishers and everyone else concerned with the production and distribution of children's literature will soon begin to take seriously the issue of sexism as well as that of racist and class bias in children's books and contribute to the still tentative but positive anti-discriminatory steps already under way.

Despite the reluctance so far of the children's book establishment and official bodies representing publishers, teachers and librarians to demonstrate their awareness of, or concern for, the issues discussed in these 'Papers . . .', there can be no doubt of the rapid growth of concern among many practising librarians and teachers, and parents and others working with children about the lack of non-biased books for children; this pamphlet should be seen as an attempt to provide some basic writings on which this concern can be sharpened and on which new strategies can be based.

USA Again? Only picture books?

As in our first 'Papers on Children's Literature', *Racist and Sexist Images in Children's Books,* the bulk of the contents of these 'Papers . . .' is made up of items originally published in the USA. The close critical attention given in the USA to the treatment of sex-roles in children's books has not yet been paralleled in Britain. In many ways, the depth and variety of the US work in this field in the English language has pre-empted similar efforts being undertaken here. At the same time, although not the most recent, the articles reprinted here are in our view the best examples of this kind of work. The article by Weitzman et al has been described as 'a model article worthy of emulation by other writers' (*School Library Journal,* USA, Jan. 1973). Czaplinski's statistical work is the most thorough content analysis of children's literature that we have come across. Lobban's article is included as the best, and so far only, British example of thorough research on sex-roles in British material, in fact British reading schemes.

It will be noted that the Weitzman and Czaplinski items are concerned with sex roles as they appear in children's picture books. Regrettably, analysis of sex roles in fiction for older children does not have the depth and comprehensiveness of the work on picture books and is not yet of sufficient quality to merit reprinting. In any case, as Weitzman points out at the beginning of her article, 'picture books play an important role in early sex-role socialization because they are a vehicle for the presentation of societal values to the young child'. We look forward to thorough studies of fiction for older children.*

The Law against Sexism

The newly passed Sex Discrimination Act has aroused a number of early

---

* A welcome recent contribution is *You're a Brick, Angela! A new look at Girls Fiction from 1839–1975* by Mary Cadogan and Patricia Craig, 1976 (Gollancz £6.50); a perceptive analysis and pretty comprehensive too, up to the 1960's. The final section on contemporary writing is weak.

hopes that the Act could be used against sexist literature, and in particular to prosecute local education authorities if they refuse to withdraw or replace the reading schemes and other children's books from their schools after it had been shown that these were sexist and discriminated against girls, i.e. by subjecting [them] . . . to detriment' (Sex Discrimination Act, 22 [c] [ii]). It is now clear that these hopes are premature. In fact there is no mention in the Act of books, school materials and the media; nor is it very realistic to expect legislation to be at the forefront of social change. Certainly no law on its own can provide all the answers or solutions. All that can be reasonably said at this very early stage is that the atmosphere and discussions surrounding the new law should be used to the utmost by parents, teachers and children to raise the issues in their neighbourhoods, schools and classrooms. The Equal Opportunities Commission *, with powers under the Act to 'conduct formal investigations' and with duties such as 'to work toward the elimination of discrimination', and 'to keep under review the working of the Sex Discrimination Act and . . . when it . . . thinks it necessary, to draw up and submit to the Secretary of State proposals for amending [it]', can be contacted by any individual or group. Certainly no opportunity should be lost in bringing to the attention of the Commission the unreasonably persistent use of sexist materials in schools or the introduction of new materials that perpetuate sexist discrimination. These are early days yet and much ground work and more research is needed before publishers and school authorities can be obliged, whether by law or public demand, to produce and distribute materials that are non-biased and non-discriminatory. We have a long way to go yet before a local education authority can be prosecuted for its use of sexist materials, such as is now happening in the USA.

Above all, in these early days, we cannot be satisfied with a mere statement of concern. For example, the Inner London Education Authority's Standing Committee on Career Opportunities for Women and Girls reported (20.11.73; Section 5.2): 'It is our view that there must be fundamental changes in the choice of material and methods from the nursery schools upwards. We have been informed of a project put into effect in Sweden, which seeks to replace early readers in which boys are invariably shown in the dominant roles with girls playing supporting parts. We feel that such a project could with advantage be considered here' and ' . . . all possible emphasis should be given in the preparation of material . . . to combat traditional attitudes and to broaden the concept of the roles of women in society'. That was over two years ago and the children of London, and everywhere else in Britain for that matter, are still waiting.

Children's Rights Workshop
April 1976

* Overseas House, Quay St., Manchester M3 3HN.

Sex-Role Socialization in Picture Books for Preschool Children

Lenore J. Weitzman, Deborah Eifler, Elizabeth Hokada and Catherine Ross

An examination of prize-winning picture books reveals that women are greatly under-represented in the titles, central roles, and illustrations. Where women do appear their characterization reinforces traditional sex-role stereotypes: boys are active while girls are passive; boys lead and rescue others while girls follow and serve others. Adult men and women are equally sex stereotyped: men engage in a wide variety of occupations while women are presented only as wives and mothers. The effects of these rigid sex-role portraits on the self image and aspirations of the developing child are discussed.

Introduction

Sex-role socialization constitutes one of the most important learning experiences for the young child. By the time the child enters kindergarten, he or she is able to make sex-role distinctions and express sex-role preferences. Boys already identify with masculine roles, and girls with feminine roles (Brown 1956). They also learn the appropriate behavior for both boys and girls and men and women. Hartley (1960) reports that, by the time they are four, children realize that the primary feminine role is housekeeping, while the primary masculine role is wage earning.

1 We are indebted to William J. Goode, Kai Erikson, Alice Rossi, and Erving Goffman for their insightful comments on an earlier draft of this paper which was presented to the 1971 meeting of the American Sociological Association, Denver, Colorado.

In addition to learning sex-role identification and sex-role expectations, boys and girls are socialized to accept society's definition of the relative worth of each of the sexes and to assume the personality characteristics that are "typical" of members of each sex. With regard to relative status, they learn that boys are more highly valued than girls. And, with regard to personality differences, they learn that boys are active and achieving while girls are passive and emotional. Eight-year-old boys describe girls as clean, neat, quiet, gentle, and fearful, while they describe adult women as unintelligent, ineffective, unadventurous, nasty, and exploitative (Hartley 1959). Indeed, Maccoby finds that, although girls begin life as better achievers than boys, they gradually fall behind as they become socialized (Maccoby 1966).

In this paper we wish to concentrate on one aspect of sex-role socialization: the socialization of preschool children through picture books. Picture books play an important role in early sex-role socialization because they are a vehicle for the presentation of societal values to the young child. Through books, children learn about the world outside of their immediate environment: they learn about what other boys and girls do, say, and feel; they learn about what is right and wrong; and they learn what is expected of children their age. In addition, books provide children with role models—images of what they can and should be like when they grow up.

Children's books reflect cultural values and are an important instrument for persuading children to accept those values. They also contain role prescriptions which encourage the child to conform to acceptable standards of behavior. The Child Study Association (1969), aware of the socialization potential of books, states that a book's emotional and intellectual impact on a young reader must be considered. Therefore it recommends that children's books present positive ethical values.

Because books for young children explicitly articulate the prevailing cultural values, they are an especially useful indicator of societal norms.[2] McClelland (1961) used children's books as indicators of achievement values in his cross-cultural study of economic development. In the period prior to increased economic development he found a high incidence of achievement motivation reflected in the children's books. This indicated a strong positive relationship between achievement imagery in children's

---

[2] Erving Goffman has questioned the direct relationship we have postulated between the themes in children's literature and societal values. He suggests that literary themes may provide alternative cultural norms or irrelevant fantasy outlets. Unfortunately, we do not know of any research other than McClelland's (1961) supporting either our own formulation or Goffman's.

stories and subsequent economic growth. McClelland (1961, p. 71) noted that the stories had provided children with clear "instructive" messages about normative behavior. Margaret Mead also commented that "a culture has to get its values across to its children in such simple terms that even a behavioral scientist can understand them."[3]

Study Design

Our study focuses on picture books for the preschool child. These books are often read over and over again at a time when children are in the process of developing their own sexual identities. Picture books are read to children when they are most impressionable, before other socialization influences (such as school, teachers, and peers) become more important at later stages in the child's development.

We have chosen to examine how sex roles are treated in those children's books identified as the "very best": the winners of the Caldecott Medal. The Caldecott Medal is given by the Children's Service Committee of the American Library Association for the most distinguished picture book of the year. The medal is the most coveted prize for preschool books. Books on the list of winners (and runners-up) are ordered by practically all children's libraries in the United States. Teachers and educators encourage children to read the Caldecotts, and conscientious parents skim the library shelves looking for those books that display the impressive gold seal which designates the winners. The Caldecott award often means sales of 60,000 books for the publisher, and others in the industry look to the winners for guidance in what to publish (Nilsen 1970).

Although we have computed a statistical analysis of all the Caldecott winners from the inception of the award in 1938, we have concentrated our intensive analysis on the winners and runners-up for the past five years. Most of the examples cited in this paper are taken from the 18 books in this latter category.[4]

In the course of our investigation we read several hundred picture books and feel that we can assert, with confidence, that our findings are applicable to the wide range of picture books. In fact, the Caldecott winners are clearly less stereotyped than the average book, and do not include the

[3] As quoted in McClelland (1961, p. 71).

[4] The Caldecott winners and runners-up for the past five years are: 1967 winner (Ness 1967), 1967 runner-up (Emberley 1967b); 1968 winner (Emberley 1967a), 1968 runners-up (Lionni 1967; Yashimo 1967; Yolen 1967); 1969 winner (Ronsome 1968), 1969 runner-up (Dayrell 1968); 1970 winner (Steig 1969), 1970 runners-up (Keats 1969; Lionni 1969; Preston 1969; Turkle 1969; Zemach 1969); 1971 winner (Haley 1970), 1971 runners-up (Sleater 1970; Lobel 1970; Sendak 1970).

7

most blatant examples of sexism.

In order to assure ourselves of the representativeness of our study, we have also examined three other groups of childrens books: the Newbery Award winners, the Little Golden Books, and the "prescribed behavior" or etiquette books.

The Newbery Award is given by the American Library Association for the best book for school-age children. Newbery books are for children who can read, and are therefore directed to children in the third to sixth grades.

The Little Golden Books we have sampled are the best sellers in children's books, since we have taken only those Little Golden Books that sold over three million copies.[5] These books sell for 39 cents in grocery stores, Woolworth's, Grant's, and toy and game stores. Consequently, they reach a more broadly based audience than do the more expensive Caldecott winners.

The last type of book we studied is what we call the "prescribed behavior" or etiquette book. Whereas other books only imply sex-role prescriptions, these books are explicit about the proper behavior for boys and girls. They also portray adult models and advise children on future roles and occupations.[6]

If we may anticipate our later findings, we would like to note here that the findings from the latter three samples strongly parallel those from the Caldecott sample. Although the remainder of this paper will be devoted primarily to the Caldecott sample, we will use some of the other books for illustrative purposes.

The Invisible Female

It would be impossible to discuss the image of females in children's books without first noting that, in fact, women are simply invisible. We found that females were underrepresented in the titles, central roles, pictures, and stories of every sample of books we examined. Most children's books are about boys, men, and male animals, and most deal exclusively with male adventures. Most pictures show men—singly or in groups. Even when women can be found in the books, they often play insignificant roles, remaining both inconspicuous and nameless.

A tabulation of the distribution of illustrations in the picture books is

---

[5] We wish to thank Robert Garlock, product manager of Little Golden Books, for his help with this information and for furnishing many of the books themselves.

[6] The Dr. Suess books, although popular among preschool audiences, were not included as a supplementary sample because they represent only one author and one publisher rather than a more broadly based series. They do, however, conform to the general pattern of sex-role portrayal that we found among the Caldecott winners.

probably the single best indicator of the importance of men and women in these books. Because women comprise 51% of our population, if there were no bias in these books they should be presented in roughly half of the pictures. However, in our sample of 18 Caldecott winners and runners-up in the past five years we found 261 pictures of males compared with 23 pictures of females. This is a ratio of 11 pictures of males for every one picture of a female. If we include animals with obvious identities, the bias is even greater. The ratio of male to female animals is 95:1.[7]

Turning to the titles of the Caldecott Medal winners since the award's inception in 1938, we find that the ratio of titles featuring males to those featuring females is 8:3.[8] Despite the presence of the popular *Cinderella, Snow White, Hansel and Gretel,* and *Little Red Riding Hood* in the sample of Golden Books that have sold more than three million copies, we find close to a 3:1 male/female ratio in this sample.[9] The 49 books that have received the Newbery Award since 1922 depict more than three males to every one female.[10]

Children scanning the list of titles of what have been designated as the very best children's books are bound to receive the impression that girls are not very important because no one has bothered to write books about them. The content of the books rarely dispels this impression.

In close to one-third of our sample of recent Caldecott books, there are no women at all. In these books, both the illustrations and the stories reflect a man's world. *Drummer Hoff* (Emberly 1967a) is about a group of army officers getting ready to fire a cannon; *Frog and Toad* (Lobel

---

[7] The illustrations of Caldecott winners and runners-up since 1967 included 166 male people, 22 female people, and 57 pictures of both males and females together. The animal illustrations included 95 of male animals, one of a female animal, and 12 of both male and female animals together. Together, this resulted in a total male/female ratio of 11:1. There were also 14 illustrations of characters without a sex.

[8] The statistics for titles of the Caldecott winners from the inception of the award in 1938 show eight titles with male names, three with female names, one with both a male and a female name together, and 22 titles without names of either sex. This resulted in an 8:3 male/female ratio. The statistics for titles of recent Caldecott winners and runners-up (since 1967) show eight titles with male names, one with a female name, one with both together, and 10 titles without names of either sex. This resulted in an 8:1 male/female ratio.

[9] The statistics for the titles of the Little Golden Books selling over three million copies show nine titles with male names, four with female names, one with both together, and 14 titles without the names of either sex. This resulted in a 9:4 male-female ratio.

[10] The statistics for the titles of Newbery winners since the inception of the award in 1922 show 20 titles with males names, six titles with female names, none with both, and 23 titles without the names of either sex. This resulted in a 10:3 male/female ratio.

1970) relates the adventures of two male animal friends; *In the Night Kitchen* (Sendak 1970) follows a boy's fantasy adventures through a kitchen that has three cooks, all of whom are male; *Frederick* (Lionni 1967) is a creative male mouse who enables his brothers to survive the cold winter; and *Alexander* is a mouse who helps a friend transform himself.

Maurice Sendak, *In the Night Kitchen*

When there are female characters, they are usually insignificant or inconspicuous. The one girl in *Goggles* (Keats 1969) is shown playing quietly in a corner. The wife in *The Sun and the Moon* (Dayrell 1968) helps by carrying wood but never speaks. There are two women in *The Fool of the World* (Ronsome 1968): the mother, who packs lunch for her sons and waves goodby, and the princess whose hand in marriage is the object of the Fool's adventures. The princess is shown only twice: once peering out of the window of the castle, and the second time in the wedding scene in which the reader must strain to find her. She does not have anything to say throughout the adventure, and of course she is not consulted in the choice of her husband; on the last page, however, the narrator assures us that she soon "loved him to distraction." Loving, watching, and helping are among the few activities allowed to women in picture books.

It is easy to imagine that the little girl reading these books might be deprived of her ego and her sense of self. She may be made to feel that girls are vacuous creatures who are less worthy and do less exciting things than men. No wonder, then, that the child psychologists report that girls at every age are less likely to identify with the feminine role, while boys of every age are more likely to identify with the masculine role (Brown 1956).

Although there is much variation in plot among the picture books, a significant majority includes some form of male adventure. The fisherman in *Seashore Story* (Yashimo 1967) rides a turtle to a hidden world under the sea. After an encounter with a lion, Sylvester is transformed into a rock in *Sylvester and the Magic Pebble* (Steig 1969). *Goggles* (Keats 1969) tells of the adventures of Peter and his friends escaping from the big boys. In *Thy Friend, Obadiah* (Turkle 1969), Obadiah rescues a sea gull; the Spider Man outfoxes the gods in *A Story, a Story* (Haley 1970). A boy rescues his girlfriend from the moon god in *The Angry Moon* (Sleator 1970). The male central characters engage in many exciting and heroic adventures which emphasize their cleverness.

In our sample of the Caldecott winners and runners-up in the last five years, we found only two of the 18 books were stories about girls.[11] In one of these stories, *Sam, Bangs, and Moonshine* (Ness 1967), the girl has a boy's name. In the second, *The Emperor and the Kite* (Yolen 1967), the heroine is a foreign princess.

Each of these girls does engage in an adventure. Sam's adventure takes place in her daydreams, while the adventure of the princess Djeow Seow occurs when her father's kingdom is seized by evil men. Like the male central characters who engage in rescues, Djeow Seow manages to save

[11] The statistics for central characters in the Caldecott winners since 1938 show 14 males, 10 females, 6 males and females together, and 4 central characters without a sex. This results in a 7:5 male/female ratio. It is important to note that the situation is becoming worse, not better. During the last five years the ratio of male to female central characters has increased. The statistics for central characters in Caldecott winners and runners-up during the last five years show a 7:2 male/female ratio in contrast to an 11:9 male/female ratio for the years prior to 1967. The statistics for central characters in the Newbery winners since 1922 show 31 males, 11 females, 4 males and females together, and 3 central characters without a sex. This results in a 3:1 male/female ratio. The statistics for central characters in the Little Golden Books selling over three million copies show an 8:3 ratio of male/female people, a 5:2 ratio of male/female animals, and a 5:3 ratio of all males and females together.

her father, but she accomplishes this task only by being so tiny and inconspicuous that the evil men do not notice her. Although Djeow Seow is one of the two women central characters, the message conveyed to readers seems to be that a girl can only triumph by playing the traditional feminine role. Women who succeed are those who are unobstrusive and work quietly behind the scenes. Women who succeed are little and inconspicuous—as are most women in picture books. Even heroines remain "invisible" females.

The Activities of Boys and Girls

We can summarize our first findings about differences in the activities of boys and girls by noting that in the world of picture books boys are active and girls are passive. Not only are boys presented in more exciting and adventuresome roles, but they engage in more varied pursuits and demand more independence. The more riotous activity is reserved for the boys. Mickey, the hero of *In the Night Kitchen* (Sendak 1970), is tossed through the air and skips from bread to dough, punching and pounding. Then he makes an airplane and flies out into the night and dives, swims, and slides until he is home again. Similarly, Archie and Peter race, climb, and hide in the story of Goggles (Keats 1969). Obadiah travels to the wharf in the cold of Massachusetts winter, and Sylvester searches for rocks in the woods.

In contrast, most of the girls in the picture books are passive and immobile. Some of them are restricted by their clothing—skirts and dresses are soiled easily and prohibit more adventuresome activities. In *The Fool of the World and the Flying Ship* (Ronsome 1968), the hero, the Fool, is dressed in a sensible manner, one which does not inhibit his movement in the tasks he has to accomplish. The princess, however, for whom all the exploits are waged, remains no more than her long gown allows her to be: a prize, an unrealistic passive creature symbolizing the reward for male adventuresomeness.

A second difference between the activities of boys and girls is that the girls are more often found indoors.[12] This places another limitation on the activities and potential adventures of girls. Even Sam, in *Sam, Bangs, and Moonshine* (Ness 1967), stays inside as she directs the activity of the book. Sam constructs a fantasy world and sends Thomas, a little boy, on wild goose chases to play out her fantasies. It is Thomas who rides the

---

[12] The statistics for activities of boys and girls in Caldecott winners since 1967 show 48 male characters indoors, 105 male characters outdoors, 15 females indoors, and 26 females outdoors. This means that 32.6% of the males are shown indoors, while 36.5% of the females are shown indoors.

Evaline Ness, *Sam, Bangs, and Moonshine*

bicycle and climbs the trees and rocks in response to Sam's fantasy. Sam, however, waits for Thomas at home, looking out the windows or sitting on the steps. Similarly, in the *Fool of the World* (Ronsome 1968), the princess remains peering out the window of her castle, watching all the activities on her behalf. While boys play in the real world outdoors, girls sit and watch them—cut off from that world by the window, porch, or fence around their homes. This distinction parallels Erik Erikson's (1964) conception of the masculine outer space and the feminine inner space.

Our third observation deals with the service activities performed by the girls who remain at home. Even the youngest girls in the stories play traditional feminine roles, directed toward pleasing and helping their brothers and fathers. Obadiah's sisters cook in the kitchen as he sits at the table sipping hot chocolate after his adventures. In *The Emperor and the Kite* (Yolen 1967), the emperor's daughters bring food to the emperor's table, but their brothers rule the kingdom.

While girls serve, boys lead.[13] Drummer Hoff, although only a boy, plays the crucial role in the final firing of the cannon. Lupin, the Indian boy in *The Angry Moon* (Sleator 1970), directs the escape from the moon god. He leads Lapowinsa, a girl exactly his size and age, every step of the way. Even at the end of the story, after the danger of the Angry Moon is past, Lupin goes down the ladder first "so that he could catch Lapowinsa if she should slip."

Training for a dependent passive role may inhibit a girl's chances for intellectual or creative success. It is likely that the excessive dependency encouraged in girls contributes to the decline in their achievement which becomes apparent as they grow older. Maccoby (1966, p. 35) has found that "For both sexes, there is a tendency for more passive-dependent children to perform poorly on a variety of intellectual tasks, and for independent children to excel."

The rescues featured in many stories require independence and self-confidence. Once again, this is almost exclusively a male activity.[14] Little boys rescue girls or helpless animals. Lupin saves a crying Lapowinsa from the flames. Obadiah saves the seagull from a rusty fishhook, and Alexander saves Willie, the windup mouse, from the fate of becoming a "tossed-out toy." In *Frederick,* Frederick's creativeness helps to spare his companions from the worst conditions of winter. In *Sam, Bangs, and Moonshine* (Ness 1967), Sam does not play the role of the rescuer although she is the central character. Rather, her father must step in and rescue Thomas and Bangs from drowning. In the end, Sam herself "must be" saved from the potential consequences of her fantasy.

Finally, we want to note the sense of camaraderie that is encouraged among boys through their adventures. For example, *The Fool of the World* depends upon the help and talents of his male companions. In *Goggles* (Keats 1969), the two male companions together outwit a gang of older boys. Similarly, the bonds of masculine friendship are stressed by Alexander, Frederick, and Frog and Toad.

---

[13] The statistics for activities of boys and girls in Caldecott winners and runners-up since 1967 show a 0:3 ratio of males/females in service functions, and a 3:2 ratio of males/females in leadership functions.

[14] The statistics for activities of boys and girls in Caldecott winners and runners-up since 1967 show a 5:1 ratio of males/females in rescue functions.

In contrast, one rarely sees only girls working or playing together. Although in reality women spend much of their time with other women, picture books imply that women cannot exist without men. The role of most of the girls is defined primarily in relation to that of the boys and men in their lives.[15] It is interesting to note that Sam turns to a boy, not a girl, to accomplish all of the activity of her fantasies. Her dreams would have no reality without Thomas.

The sex differences we have noted are even more apparent in the prescriptive or etiquette books. An excellent example is found in a pair of matched books: *The Very Little Boy* (Krasilovsky 1962a) and *The Very Little Girl* (Krasilovsky 1962b). Both books are written by the same author, follow the same format, and teach the same lesson: that little children grow up to be big children. However, the maturation process differs sharply for the very little boy and the very little girl.[16]

As we open to the first pages of the *Very Little Boy* (Krasilovsky 1962a) we find the boy playing on the living room floor by the fireplace. He has already discarded a big rubber ball and is now making a racket by banging on a pan with a spoon. In contrast, the first page of the *Very Little Girl* (Krasilovsky 1962b) shows the little girl sitting quietly in a big chair. There is no activity in the picture: the little girl is doing nothing but sitting with her hands folded in her lap. This is our introduction to an angelic little girl and a boisterous little boy.

In the following pages the author compares the size of the children to the objects around them; we find that the boy is smaller than a cornstalk, his baseball bat, his sled, his father's workbench, and a lawnmower. In contrast, the little girl is smaller than the rosebush, a kitchen stool, and her mother's workbasket. We note that the boy will be interested in sports—in fact, both the basketball and sled are *his,* waiting there for him until he is old enough to use them. The girl has been given no comparable presents by her parents. She can only look forward to conquering the rosebush and the kitchen stool.

---

[15] This problem is not confined to children's books. As Virginia Woolf pointed out over 40 years ago, women in literature are rarely represented as friends: "They are now and then mothers and daughters. But almost without exception they are shown in their relation to men. It was strange to think that all the great women of fiction were, until Jane Austen's day, . . . seen only in relation to the other sex. And how little can a man know even of that when he observes it through the black or rosy spectacles which sex puts upon his nose. Hence, perhaps the particular nature of women in fiction; the astonishing extremes of her beauty and horror" (1929, p. 86).

[16] We gratefully acknowledge Barbara Fried's imaginative analysis of these two books in her paper, "What Our Children Are Reading," written for Sociology 62a, Yale University, fall term, 1970.

Phyllis Krasilovsky, *The Very Little Boy, The Very Little Girl,*
illustrated by Ninon

Even more important is the way in which each of them relates to these objects. The little boy is in constant motion, continuously interacting with the world around him. He is *jumping* up to touch the scarecrow next to the cornstalk, *unwrapping* his baseball bat (leaving the mess of paper, string, and box for someone else to clean up), *building* blocks on top of his sled, *reaching* up on tiptoe to touch his father's workbench, and *spraying* the lawn (and himself) with the garden hose. In contrast, the little girl relates to each of the objects around her merely by *looking* at them.

Similarly, when the author indicates what each child is too small to do, we find that the little boy is too small to engage in a series of adventures. The little girl, however, is too small to *see* things from the sidelines. Thus, we are told that the little boy is too small to *march* in the parade, to *feed* the elephant at the zoo, and to *touch* the pedals on his bike. But the little girl is too small to *see* over the garden fence and to *see* the face on the grandfather clock. Even when the little girl is trying to see something she appears to be posing, and thus looks more like a doll than a curious little girl.

The little girl's clothes indicate that she is not meant to be active. She wears frilly, starchy, pink dresses, and her hair is always neatly combed and tied with ribbons. She looks pretty—too pretty to ride a bike, play ball, or visit the zoo.

Little girls are often pictured as pretty dolls who are not meant to do anything but be admired and bring pleasure. Their constant smile teaches that women are meant to please, to make others smile, and be happy. This image may reflect parental values. In a study of the attitudes of middle-class fathers toward their children, Aberle and Naegele (1960, pp. 188–98) report that the parent satisfaction with their daughters seemed to focus on their daughters being nice, sweet, pretty, affectionate, and well liked.

If we follow the little boy and little girl as they grow up, we can watch the development of the proper service role in a little woman. We are shown that the girl grows big enough to water the rosebush, stir the cake batter, set the table, play nurse, and help the doctor (who is, of course, a boy), pick fruit from the trees, take milk from the refrigerator, prepare a baby's formula, and feed her baby brother. Conveniently enough for their future husbands, girls in storybooks learn to wash, iron, hang up clothes to dry, cook, and set the table. Of course, when the boy grows up, he engages in more active pursuits: he catches butterflies, mows the lawn, marches in the parade, visits the zoo to feed the elephants, and hammers wood at the workbench.

One particularly striking contrast between the two children is illustrated by the pictures of both of them with their dogs. In discussing how both have matured, the author tells us that both have grown up to be bigger than their pets. The picture of the little girl, however, makes us seriously doubt any grown-up self-confidence and authority. She is shown being pulled by a very small dog, whom she obviously cannot control. The little boy, in contrast, is in firm command of a much bigger dog, and does not even need a leash to control him.

It is easy to see why many little girls prefer to identify with the male role (Hartup 1962; Brown 1956). The little girl who does find the male role more attractive is faced with a dilemma. If she follows her desires and behaves like a tomboy, she may be criticized by her parents and teachers. On the other hand, if she gives up her yearnings and identities with the traditional feminine role, she will feel stifled. Girls who wish to be more than placid and pretty are left without an acceptable role alternative. They must choose between alienation from their own sex of assignment, and alienation from their real behavioral and temperamental preferences.

The rigidity of sex-role stereotypes is not harmful only to little girls. Little boys may feel equally constrained by the necessity to be fearless, brave, and clever at all times. While girls are allowed a great deal of emotional expression, a boy who cries or expresses fear is unacceptable.[17] Just as the only girls who are heroines in picture books have boys' names or are foreign princesses, the only boys who cry in picture books are animals—frogs and toads and donkeys.

The price of the standardization and rigidity of sex roles is paid by children of both sexes. Eleanor Maccoby (1966, p. 35) has reported that analytic thinking, creativity, and general intelligence are associated with cross-sex typing. Thus, rigid sex-role definitions not only foster unhappiness in children but they also hamper the child's fullest intellectual and social development.

Role Models: Adult Men and Women

Adult role models provide another crucial component of sex-role socialization. By observing adult men and women, boys and girls learn what will be expected of them when they grow older. They are likely to identify with adults of the same sex, and desire to be like them. Thus, role models not only present children with future images of themselves but they also influence a child's aspirations and goals.

We found the image of the adult woman to be stereotyped and limited.

---

[17] But Hartley (1959) also discovered that as a corollary the boys felt extreme pressure as a result of the rigid masculine role prescriptions which they saw as demanding that they be strong, intelligent, and generally successful. The boys believed that adults liked girls better because the girls were cute and well behaved.

Once again, the females are passive while the males are active. Men predominate in the outside activities while more of the women are inside. In the house, the women perform almost exclusively service functions, taking care of the men and children in their families. When men lead, women follow. When men rescue others, women are the rescued.[18]

Brinton Turkle, *Thy Friend, Obadiah*

In most of the stories, the sole adult woman is identified only as a mother or a wife. Obadiah's mother cooks, feeds him hot chocolate, and goes to church. The wife of the Sun God carries wood to help him build the house, but she never speaks. Sylvester's mother is shown sweeping, packing a picnic lunch, knitting, and crying. And Mrs. Noah, who had an important role in the biblical story of the flood, is completely omitted from the children's book version.

The remaining three roles that women play are also exclusively feminine roles: one is a fairy, the second a fairy godmother, and the third an underwater maiden. The fairy godmother is the only adult female who plays an active leadership role. The one nonstereotyped woman is clearly not a

[18] Among the Caldecott winners and runners-up for the past five years, we found that women were engaged in a much narrower range of activities then men. The ratio of male to female adults engaged in service activities was 1:7, while the ratio of male to female adults in leadership activities was 5:0, and the ratio of the male to female adults in rescue activities was 4:1. In addition, 40% of adult females, but only 31% of adult males, were pictured indoors.

"normal" woman—she is a mythical creature.

In contrast to the limited range in women's roles, the roles that men play are varied and interesting. They are storekeepers, housebuilders, kings, spiders, storytellers, gods, monks, fighters, fishermen, policemen, soldiers, adventurers, fathers, cooks, preachers, judges, and farmers.

Perhaps our most significant finding was that *not one* woman in the Caldecott sample had a job or profession. In a country where 40% of the women are in the labor force, and close to 30 million women work, it is absurd to find that women in picture books remain only mothers and wives (U.S. Department of Labor 1969). In fact, 90% of the women in this country will be in the labor force at some time in their lives.

Motherhood is presented in picture books as a full-time, lifetime job, although for most women it is in reality a part-time 10-year commitment. The changing demographic patterns in this country indicate that

William Steig, *Sylvester and the Magic Pebble*

the average woman has completed the main portion of her childrearing by her mid-thirties and has 24 more productive years in the labor force if she returns to work once her children are in school. Today even the mothers of young children work. There are over 10 million of them currently in the labor force (U.S. Department of Labor 1969, p. 39).

As the average woman spends even less time as a mother in the future, it is unrealistic for picture books to present the role of mother as the only possible occupation for the young girl. Alice Rossi (1964, p. 105) has noted that today the average girl may spend as many years with her dolls as the average mother spends with her children.

The way in which the motherhood role is presented in children's books is also unrealistic. She is almost always confined to the house, although she is usually too well dressed for housework. Her duties are not portrayed as difficult or challenging—she is shown as a housebound servant who cares for her husband and children. She washes dishes, cooks, vacuums, yells at the children, cleans up, does the laundry, and takes care of babies. For example, a typical domestic scene in *Sylvester and the Magic Pebble* shows the father reading the paper, Sylvester playing with his rock collection, and the mother sweeping the floor.

The picture books do not present a realistic picture of what real mothers do. Real mothers drive cars, read books, vote, take children on trips, balance checkbooks, engage in volunteer activities, ring doorbells canvassing, raise money for charity, work in the garden, fix things in the house, are active in local politics, belong to the League of Women Voters and the PTA, etc.[19]

Nor do these picture books provide a realistic image of fathers and husbands. Fathers never help in the mundane duties of child care. Nor do husbands share the dishwashing, cooking, cleaning, or shopping. From these stereotyped images in picture books, little boys may learn to expect their wives to do all the housework and to cater to their needs. These unreal expectations of marriage will inevitably bring disappointment and discontent to both the male and the female partners.

Lonnie Carton's two books, *Mommies* (1960b) and *Daddies* (1960a), are excellent examples of the contrasting lives to which boys and girls can look forward if they follow the role models provided by the adult characters in picture books. As the books begin, Mommy puts on her apron to prepare for a day of homemaking, while Daddy dashes out of the house with his briefcase on the way to work. The next two pages show the real

---

[19] Only one of the Caldecott winners presents the woman as an active equal to her husband. It is Edna Mitchell Preston's *Pop Corn and Ma Goodness* (1969)

differences between the woman's world and the man's world. Daddies are shown as carpenters, executives, house painters, mailmen, teachers, cooks, and storekeepers. They are also the bearers of knowledge.

> Daddies drive the trucks and cars,
> The buses, boats and trains.
> Daddies build the roads and bridges,
> Houses, stores and planes.
> Daddies work in factories and
> Daddies make the things grow.
> Daddies work to figure out
> The things we do not know (1960).

On the corresponding two pages (in *Mommies*), we learn that, although the mother supposedly does "lots and lots," her tasks consist of washing dishes, scrubbing pots and walls, cooking, baking, tying shoes, catching balls, and answering questions (which seems to be her most "creative" role so far). Mommy does leave the house several times but only to shop for groceries or to take the children out to play. (She does drive a car in this book, however, which is unusual.)

In contrast, when Daddy comes home he not only plays in a more exciting way with the children but he provides their contact with the outside world. While Mommies are restrictive, and "shout if you play near the street," Daddies take you on trips in cars, buses, and trains; Daddies take you to the circus, park, and zoo; buy you ice cream; and teach you to swim. Daddies also understand you better because they "know you're big enough and brave enough to do lots of things that mommies think are much too hard for you." Mothers, however, are useful for taking care of you when you are sick, cleaning up after you, and telling you what to do. Mommies do smile, hug, comfort, and nurture, but they also scold and instruct in a not altogether pleasant manner. They tell you to be quiet, and to "Sit still and eat!" Ironically, this negative image of the nagging mother may be a result of an exclusive devotion to motherhood. As Alice Rossi has observed: "If a woman's adult efforts are concentrated exclusively on her children, she is likely more to stifle than broaden her children's perspective and preparation for adult life. . . . In myriad ways the mother binds the child to her, dampening his initiative, resenting his growing independence in adolescence, creating a subtle dependence which makes it difficult for the child to achieve full adult stature" (1964, p. 113).

In addition to having a negative effect on children, this preoccupation with motherhood may also be harmful to the mother herself. Pauline Bart (1970, p. 72) has reported extreme depression among middle-aged women who have been overinvolved with and have overidentified with their children.

We have already noted that there are no working women in the Caldecott sample. It is no disparagement of the housewife or mother to point out that alternative roles are available to, and chosen by, many women and that girls can be presented with alternative models so that they, like boys, may be able to think of a wide range of future options.

Because there are no female occupational role models in the Caldecott books, we will turn to the prescribed role books to examine the types of occupations that are encouraged for boys and girls. For this analysis we will compare a very popular pair of Hallmark matched books: *What Boys Can Be* (Walley, n.d., *a*) and *What Girls Can be* (Walley, n.d., *b*). Both books follow the same format: each page shows a boy or a girl playing an occupational role. We are told that boys can be:

> *a fireman* who squirts water on the flames, and
> *a baseball* player who wins lots of games.
> *a bus driver* who helps people travel far, or
> *a policeman* with a siren in his car.
> *a cowboy* who goes on cattle drives, and
> *a doctor* who helps to save people's lives.
> *a sailor* on a ship that takes you everywhere, and
> *a pilot* who goes flying through the air.
> *a clown* with silly tricks to do, and
> a pet tiger owner who *runs the zoo*.
> *a farmer* who drives a big red tractor, and
> on TV shows, if I become *an actor*.
> *an astronaut* who lives in a space station, and
> someday grow up to be *President* of the nation
> [Emphasis added; Walley, n.d., *a*]

The second book tells us that girls can be:

> *a nurse*, with white uniforms to wear, or
> *a stewardess*, who flies everywhere.
> *a ballerina*, who dances and twirls around, or
> *a candy shop owner*, the best in town.
> *a model*, who wears lots of pretty clothes,
> *a big star* in the movies and on special TV shows
> *a secretary* who'll type without mistakes, or
> *an artist*, painting trees and clouds and lakes.
> *a teacher in nursery school* some day, or
> *a singer* and make records people play.
> *a designer of dresses* in the very latest style, or
> *a bride*, who comes walking down the aisle.
> *a housewife*, someday when I am grown, and
> *a mother*, with some children of my own
> [Emphasis added; Walley, n.d., *b*]

The two concluding pictures are the most significant; the ultimate goal for which little boys are to aim is nothing less than the president of the nation. For girls, the comparable pinnacle of achievement is motherhood!

Many of the differences in the occupations in these two books parallel the male/female differences we have already noted. One is the inside/outside distribution. Eleven of the female occupations are shown being performed inside, while only three are outside. Indeed, none of the female occupations listed necessitates being performed outdoors. The ratio for the male occupations is exactly reversed: three are inside, 11 outside.

We already observed that little girls are encouraged to succeed by looking pretty and serving others. It should therefore not be surprising to find that the women are concentrated in glamorous and service occupations. The most prestigious feminine occupations are those in which a girl can succeed only if she is physically attractive. The glamour occupations of model and movie star are the two most highly rewarded among the female choices. Since few women can ever achieve high status in these glamorous professions, the real message in these books is that women's true function lies in service. Service occupations, such as nurse, secretary, housewife, mother, and stewardess, reinforce the traditional patterns to feminine success.

Although some of the male occupations also require physical attractiveness (actor) and service (bus driver), there is a much greater range of variation in the other skills they require: baseball players need athletic ability, policemen are supposed to be strong and brave, pilots and doctors need brains, astronauts need mechanical skills and great energy, clowns must be clever and funny, and presidents need political acumen.

If we compare the status level of the male and female occupations, it is apparent that men fill the most prestigious and highly paid positions. They are the doctors, pilots, astronauts, and presidents. Even when men and women are engaged in occupations in the same field, it is the men who hold the positions which demand the most skill and leadership. While men are doctors, women are nurses; while men are pilots, women are stewardesses. Only one of the women is engaged in a professional occupation: the teacher. It is important to note, however, that the authors carefully specified that she was a *nursery school teacher.*

Similarly, most of the occupations that require advanced education are occupied by men. Four of the males have apparently gone to college, compared with only one of the women.

It is clear that the book *What Boys Can Be* encourages a little boy's career ambitions. He is told that he has the potential for achieving any of the exciting and highly rewarded occupations in our society.

In contrast, the book *What Girls Can Be* tells the little girl that she can have ambitions if she is pretty. Her potential for achieving a prestigious and rewarding job is dependent on her physical attributes. If she is not attractive, she must be satisfied with a life of mundane service. No women are represented in traditional male occupations, such as doctor, lawyer, engineer, or scientist. With women comprising 7% of the country's physicians and 4% of its lawyers, surely it is more probable that a girl will achieve one of these professional statuses than it is that a boy will become president.

The occupational distribution presented in these books is even worse than the real inequitable distribution of employment in the professions. Picture books could inspire children to strive for personal and occupational goals that would take them beyond their everyday world. Instead women are denied both the due recognition for their present achievements and the encouragement to aspire to more broadly defined possibilities in the future.

Conclusion

Preschool children invest their intellects and imaginations in picture books at a time when they are forming their self-images and future expectations. Our study has suggested that the girls and women depicted in these books are a dull and stereotyped lot. We have noted that little girls receive attention and praise for their attractiveness, while boys are admired for their achievements and cleverness. Most of the women in picture books have status by virtue of their relationships to specific men—they are the wives of the kings, judges, adventurers, and explorers, but they themselves are not the rulers, judges, adventurers, and explorers.

Through picture books, girls are taught to have low aspirations because there are so few opportunities portrayed as available to them. The world of picture books never tells little girls that as women they might find fulfillment outside of their homes or through intellectual pursuits. Women are excluded from the world of sports, politics, and science. Their future occupational world is presented as consisting primarily of glamour and service. Ironically, many of these books are written by prize-winning female authors whose own lives are probably unlike those they advertise.[20]

It is clear that the storybook characters reinforce the traditional sex-role

---

[20] A tabulation of the percentage of female authors indicates that 41% of the Caldecott and 58% of the Newbery Medal winners were written by women. However, women authors appear to be more positive than their male counterparts. The pre-1967 Caldecotts, which had a larger percentage of female central characters, also have a larger percentage of female authors: 48% compared with 33%.

assumptions. Perhaps this is indicative of American preferences for creativeness and curiosity in boys and neatness and passivity in girls. Many parents want their sons to grow up to be brave and intelligent and their daughters to be pretty and compliant.

In the past, social theorists have assumed that such strongly differentiated sex roles would facilitate a child's identification with the parent of the same sex. For example, Talcott Parsons (1955) has commented that "if the boy is to identify with his father there must be discrimination in role terms between the two parents" (1955, p. 80). More recently, however, Philip Slater (1964) has argued that adult role models who exhibit stereotyped sex-role differentiation may impede, rather than facilitate, the child's sex-role identification. Children find it easier to identify with less differentiated and less stereotyped parental role models. It is easier for them to internalize parental values when nurturance (the typically feminine role) and discipline (the typically masculine role) come from the same person.

Not only do narrow role definitions impede the child's identification with the same sex parent, but rigid sex-role distinctions may actually be harmful to the normal personality development of the child. In fact, Slater (1964) has postulated a negative relationship between the child's emotional adjustment and the degree of parental role differentiation.

Some evidence, then, suggests these sex roles are rigid and possibly harmful. They discourage and restrict a woman's potential and offer her fulfillment only through the limited spheres of glamour and service. More flexible definitions of sex roles would seem to be more healthful in encouraging a greater variety of role possibilities. Stories could provide a more positive image of a woman's potential—of her physical, intellectual, creative, and emotional capabilities.

Picture books could also present a less stereotyped and less rigid definition of male roles by encouraging boys to express their emotions as well as their intellect. Books might show little boys crying, playing with stuffed toys and dolls, and helping in the house. Stereotypes could be weakened by books showing boys being rewarded for being emotional and supportive, and girls being rewarded for being intelligent and adventuresome.

Although Zelditch (1955, p. 341) has noted the cross-cultural predominance of males in instrumental roles and females in expressive roles—like the patterns we found in children's books—Slater (1964) suggests that the ability to alternate instrumental and expressive role performance rapidly—what he calls interpersonal flexibility—is coming to be more highly valued in our society.

This argues for less stereotyped adult roles. Fathers could take a more

Edna Mitchell Preston, *Pop Corn and Ma Goodness*

active role in housework and child care. And, similarly, the roles of adult women could be extended beyond the limited confines of the home, as in fact they are. When women are shown at home, they could be portrayed as the busy and creative people that many housewives are. For example, the woman in *Pop Corn and Ma Goodness*, the single exception to the Caldecott norm, equally shares diversified activities with her husband

If these books are to present real-life roles, they could give more attention to single parents and divorced families. Stories could present the real-life problems that children in these families face: visiting a divorced father, having two sets of parents, not having a father at school on father's day, or having a different name than one's mother.

The simplified and stereotyped images in these books present such a narrow view of reality that they must violate the child's own knowledge

27

of a rich and complex world.[21] Perhaps these images are motivated by the same kind of impulse that makes parents lie to their children in order to "protect" them.[22] As a result, the child is given an idealized version of the truth, rather than having his real and pressing questions answered. Not only are the child's legitimate questions ignored, but no effort is made to create a social awareness which encompasses the wider society. Picture books actually deny the existence of the discontented, the poor, the ethnic minorities, and the urban slum dwellers.

Stories have always been a means for perpetuating the fundamental cultural values and myths. Stories have also been a stimulus for fantasy imagination and achievement. Books could develop this latter quality to encourage the imagination and creativity of all children. This would provide an important implementation of the growing demand for *both* girls and boys to have a real opportunity to fulfill their human potential.

---

[21] We are indebted to William J. Goode for this insight.

[22] This is not to deny the value of fantasy. As Margaret Fuller wrote in 1855: "Children need some childish talk, some childish play, some childish books. But they also need, and need more, difficulties to overcome, and a sense of the vast mysteries which the progress of their intelligence shall aide them to unravel. This sense is naturally their delight . . . and it must not be dulled by premature explanations or subterfuges of any kind" (pp. 310–13). Alice Rossi brought this work to our attention.

References

Aberle, David F., and Kasper D. Naegele. 1960. "Middle-Class Fathers' Occupational Role and Attitudes towards Children." In *A Modern Introduction to the Family*, edited by Norman W. Bell and Ezra F. Vogel. New York: Free Press.

Bart, Pauline. 1970. "Portney's Mother's Complaint." *Trans-Action* (November/December).

Brown, Daniel G. 1956. "Sex Role Preference in Young Children." *Psychological Monograph* 70, no. 14.

Carton, Lonnie C. 1960a. *Daddies*. New York: Random House.

———. 1960b. *Mommies*. New York: Random House.

Child Study Association. 1969. *List of Recommended Books*. New York: Child Study Association.

Dayrell, Elphinstone. 1968. *Why the Sun and the Moon Live in the Sky*. Boston: Houghton Mifflin.

Emberley, Barbara. 1967a. *Drummer Hoff*. Englewood Cliffs, N.J.: Prentice-Hall. (GB Bodley Head)

———. 1967b. *One Wide River to Cross*. Englewood Cliffs, N.J.: Prentice-Hall. (GB Chatto & Windus)

Erikson, Erik H. 1964. "Inner and Outer Space: Reflections on Womanhood." *The Woman in America*, edited by Robert Jay Lifton. Boston: Houghton-Mifflin.

Fuller, Margaret. 1855. "Children's Books." In *Women in the Nineteenth Century*, by John J. Jewett. Boston.

Haley, Gail E. 1970. *A Story, a Story: An African Tale Retold*. New York: Atheneum (GB Methuen)

Hartley, Ruth E. 1959. "Sex-Role Pressures and the Socialization of the Male Child." *Psychological Reports* 5:457–68.

———. 1960. "Children's Concepts of Males and Female Roles." *Merrill-Palmer Quarterly* 6:83–91.

Hartup, Willard W. 1962. "Some Correlates of Parental Imitation in Young Children." *Child Development* 33:85–96.

Keats, Jack Ezra. 1969. *Goggles!* Toronto: Macmillan. (GB Bodley Head)

Krasilovsky, Phyllis. 1962a. *The Very Little Boy*. Illustrated by Ninon. New York Doubleday. (GB Worlds Work)

———. 1962b. *The Very Little Girl*. Illustrated by Ninon. New York: Doubleday. (GB Worlds Work)

Lionni, Leo. 1967. *Frederick*. New York: Random House. (GB Abelard Schuman)

Lobel, Arnold. 1970 *Frog and Toad Are Friends*. New York: Harper & Row. (GB Worlds Work)

McClelland, David C. 1961. *The Achieving Society*. New York: Free Press.

Maccoby, Eleanor E. 1966. "Sex Differences in Intellectual Functioning." In *The Development of Sex Differences*. Stanford, Calif.: Stanford University Press.

Ness, Evaline. 1967. *Sam, Bangs, and Moonshine*. New York: Holt, Rinehart & Winston. (GB Bodley Head)

Nilsen, Alleen Pace. 1970. "Women in Children's Literature." Paper presented at workshop on Children's Literature, Modern Language Association Meeting, December 27, New York.

Parsons, Talcott. 1955. "Family Structure and the Socialization of the Child." In *Family, Socialization and Interaction Process*, edited by Talcott Parsons and Robert F. Bales. New York: Free Press.

Preston, Edna Mitchell. 1969. *Pop Corn and Ma Goodness*. New York: Viking.

Ronsome, Arthur. 1968. *The Fool of the World and the Flying Ship* New York: Farrar, Straus & Giroux.

Rossi, Alice. 1964. "Equality between the Sexes." *The Woman in America*, edited by Robert Jay Lifton. Boston: Houghton-Mifflin.

Sendak, Maurice. 1970. *In the Night Kitchen.* New York: Harper & Row.
  (GB Bodley Head)
Slater, Philip. 1964. "Parental Role Differentiation." In *The Family: Its Structure and Functions,* edited by Rose L. Coser. New York: St. Martin's.
Sleator, William. 1970. *The Angry Moon.* Boston: Little, Brown.
Steig, William. 1969. *Sylvester and the Magic Pebble.* New York: Simon & Schuster.
  (GB Abelard Schuman)
Turkle, Brinton. 1969. *Thy Friend, Obadiah.* New York: Viking.
U.S. Department of Labor. 1969. *1969 Handbook on Women Workers.* Washington D.C.: Government Printing Office.
Walley, Dean. n.d., *a. What Boys Can be.* Kansas City: Hallmark.
———. n.d., *b. What Girls Can Be.* Kansas City: Hallmark.
Woolf, Virginia. 1929. *A Room of One's Own.* New York: Harcourt, Brace & World (GB Penguin)
Yashimo, Taro. 1967. *Seashore Story.* New York: Viking.
Yolen, Jane. 1967. *The Emperor and the Kite.* Cleveland: World.
Zelditch, Morris, Jr. 1955. "Role Differentiation in the Nuclear Family." In *Family, Socialization, and Interaction Process,* edited by Talcott Parsons and Robert F. Bales. New York: Free Press.
Zemach, Harve. 1969. *The Judge.* New York: Farrar, Strauss & Giroux.

Sexism in Award Winning Picture Books

Extracts from a 1972 thesis by Suzanne M. Czaplinski

Suzanne Czaplinski's 1972 thesis 'Sexism in Award Winning Picture Books' is the most thorough and systematic analysis of sexism in children's books that we have come across. However, due to its length we can only reprint those extracts of her thesis which demonstrate her most important evidence. For those still unconvinced about sexism in children's books – even to the extent of denying its existence – Czaplinski demonstrates by her scholarly research that children's books are indeed sexist. In the material reproduced here, Czaplinski shows that children's books are not only sexist in their under-representation of females, but also in recent years they have become more, not less sexist. We should like to thank Suzanne Czaplinski for her kind permission to reprint these extracts. Copies of her complete thesis are available from Know Inc, P O Box 86031, Pittsburg, Penn 15221, USA, price $2 plus postage.

Czaplinski chose to concentrate on award-winners and best-sellers, i.e. "books which have been given the nod not only by librarians and store owners, but because of their prestige and attractiveness, by parents and small children as well". She selected therefore Caldecott Award* winners from 1941–1971, Carroll Award** winning picture books from 1958–1971, and the New York Times Book Review of Children's Books best sellers' list*** of November 7th 1971. Five overlaps occurred between the two classes of award winners and the best sellers. Czaplinski's total sample of picture books was therefore composed of 60 separate entries.

* An annual award given to the artist of the most distinguished picture book for children published in the USA during the preceding year.
** An annual US award for books the selection committee feels to be "worthy of a place on the shelf beside the inimitable *Alice in Wonderland.*"
*** Based on reports obtained from more than 125 bookstores in 64 communities in the USA.

Extract 1 **Analyses of Characters Presented Pictorially and In Text**

The following tables show the numbers of each sex present pictorially and in the text of each book. This is determined pictorially by counting each person, sex-typed animal or inanimate object shown and placing him or her in a male or female category. When there is any question of sex, the being is not counted. The procedures for determination of the numbers of both sexes in each text is to count every page upon which a male or female is mentioned. If he or she is mentioned again on the same page, he or she is not counted, unless present in a separate passage with a different picture. Pronouns are counted once if they are the only referent on the page denoting sex. Also occupational labels are counted, if a pictorial referrent is present which determines the sex of the one occupied.

The following tables present totals of characters present pictorially and in text for the three categories of books.

Table 1 **Total per cent of males and females in Caldecott, Carroll, and bestselling books presented pictorially**

Categories	Males No	%	Females No	%	Both No	%
Caldecott Winners	1283	52	1156	48	2439	100
Carroll Winners	2143	82	489	18	2632	100
NYT Bestsellers	806	85	138	15	944	100
Entire Sampling	4232	70	1783	30	6015	100

Table 2 **Total per cent of males and females in Caldecott, Carroll, and bestselling books presented in text**

Categories	Males No	%	Females No	%	Both No	%
Caldecott Winners	870	63	517	37	1387	100
Carroll Winners	2641	82	569	18	3210	100
NYT Bestsellers	1135	91	117	9	1252	100
Entire Sampling	4646	80	1203	20	5849	100

As seen from the above two tables, the Carroll Award winners and bestsellers show a relatively consistent number of both sexes pictorially and in text. The Caldecott winners show a greater difference between pictures and text, and pictorially the numbers of each sex appears to be fairly well balanced. However, checking Table 1 we find that in *Madeline's Rescue* 427 female characters are pictured. This is an extreme figure among the Caldecott winners, with no other entry above 150 characters for either sex. For the purpose of comparison, *Madeline's Rescue* will be removed from the Caldecott winners and will result in the following totals:

Table 3 **Per cent of males and females in bestselling, Carroll, and Caldecott books presented pictorially excluding** *Madeline's Rescue*

	Males		Females		Both	
Categories	No	%	No	%	No	%
NYT Bestsellers	806	85	138	15	944	100
Carroll Winners	2143	82	489	18	2632	100
Caldecott Winners	1283	64	729	36	2012	100
Entire Sampling	4232	76	1356	24	5588	100

The percentage of male characters presented pictorially and in text is significantly greater than the percentage of female characters. Perhaps most significant is that even when female characters are pictured, they are often not mentioned in the text. As indicated by Tables 1, 2 and 3, from 24 to 30% of all characters pictured are female, but only 20% of all characters mentioned in text are female. Starring roles may be a determining factor in the above, with females being reserved for crowd scenes or supporting roles, pictured but not mentioned.

Extract 2 **Time Study**

A time study will be a helpful tool in order to indicate increase or decrease in sex bias over time. As was previously mentioned, Caldecott Awards are given the year following the date of publication. However, Carroll Awards may be given at any time following the date of publication, and bestsellers sampled cover the years 1904–1963. For the purpose of this time study, dates of publication, not award, will be considered. Consequently, some of the books sampled are placed in the category 1900–1930. The remainder of the sampling will be divided by ten year periods.

Table 4 **Per cent of male and female characters in starring roles over time**

	Males		Females		Groups		All	
Time Periods	No	%	No	%	No	%	No	%
1900–1929	5	100	0	0	0	0	5	100
1930–1939	5	83	0	0	1	17	6	100
1940–1949	4	29	3	21	7	50	14	100
1950–1959	5	41.5	5	41.5	2	17	12	100
1960–1969	16	80	3	15	1	5	20	100
1970–1972	3	100	0	0	0	0	3	100
All Periods	38	63	11	18.5	11	18.5	60	100

Table 5 **Per cent of male and female characters presented pictorially over time**

	Males		Females		Both	
Time Periods	No	%	No	%	No	%
1900–1929	796	87	119	13	915	100
1930–1939	358	85	74	15	432	100
1940–1949	781	72	301	28	1082	100
1950–1959	570	39	874	61	1444	100
1960–1969	1013	80	263	20	1276	100
1970–1972	120	70	52	30	172	100
All Periods	3638	68	1683	32	5321	100

Table 6 **Per cent of male and female characters presented in text over time**

	Males		Females		Both	
Time Periods	No	%	No	%	No	%
1900–1929	1541	82	199	18	1740	100
1930–1939	311	72	124	28	435	100
1940–1949	467	69	207	31	674	100
1950–1959	320	53	289	47	609	100
1960–1969	897	78	253	22	1150	100
1970–1972	101	64	56	36	157	100
All Periods	3637	76	1128	24	4765	100

As can be seen by the above tables, sex bias decreased during the 40's and 50's and increased overwhelmingly during the 60's. Women were more equally represented in the labor force during the 40's, the war years and immediately following, and perhaps some of their increased freedom during this period influenced the content of children's picture books. With some lag time understandable, the 50's, era of the "contented" homemaker, show their effect on children's literature by the pronounced increase in sexism during the 60's and early 70's. Starring roles over time provide us with a mirror image of the fluctuation in equality and inequality of the sexes. The following bar charts will show this more clearly. Especially after studying figure 1, it is clear that the time is very ripe for an extensive examination of children's picture books.

Total figures in Tables 5 and 6 vary from Tables 1 and 2 because overlapping award winners and bestsellers are tallied once.

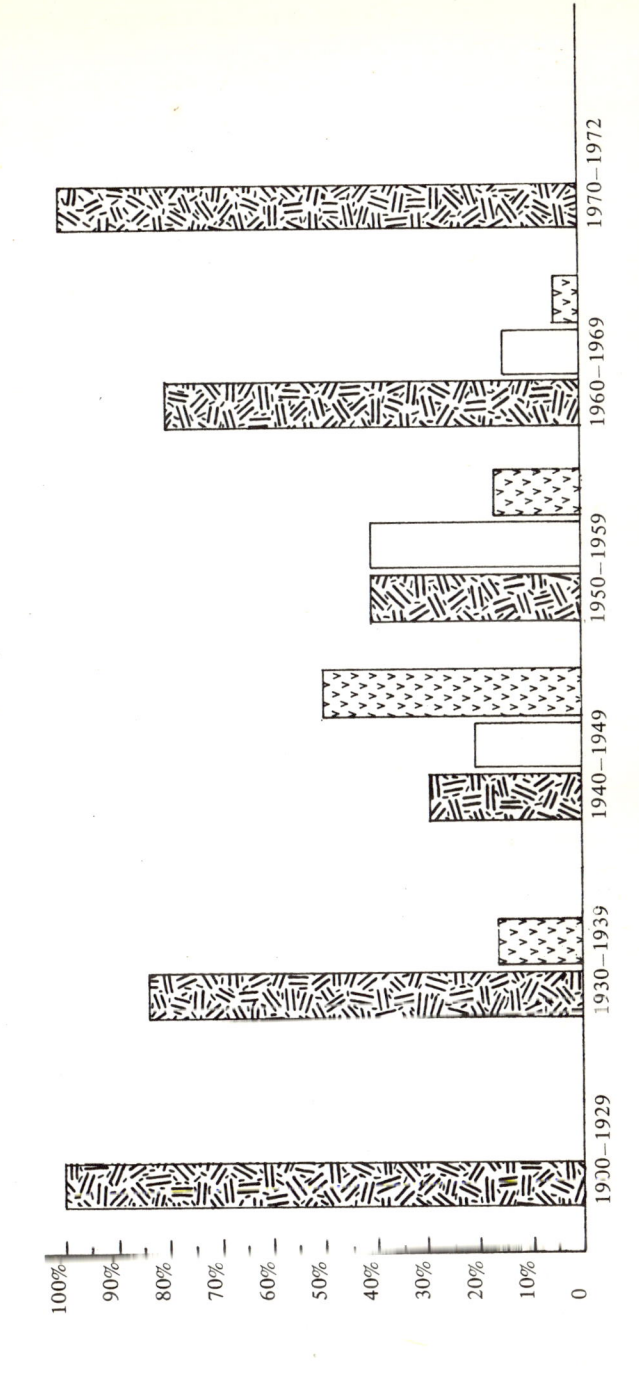

Figure 1 Per cent of males and females in starring roles of picture books over time

Figure 2 Per cent of male and female characters presented pictorially over time

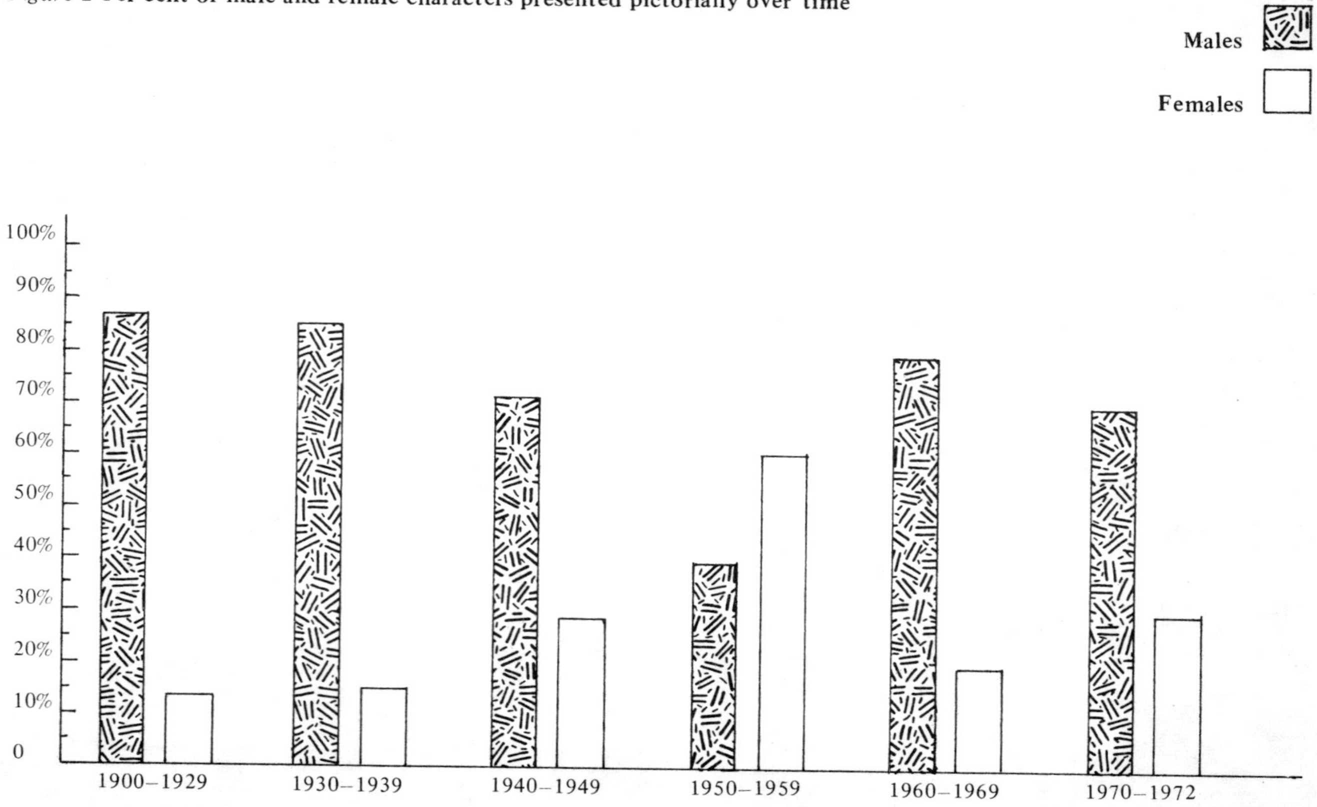

Figure 3 **Per cent of male and female characters presented in text over time**

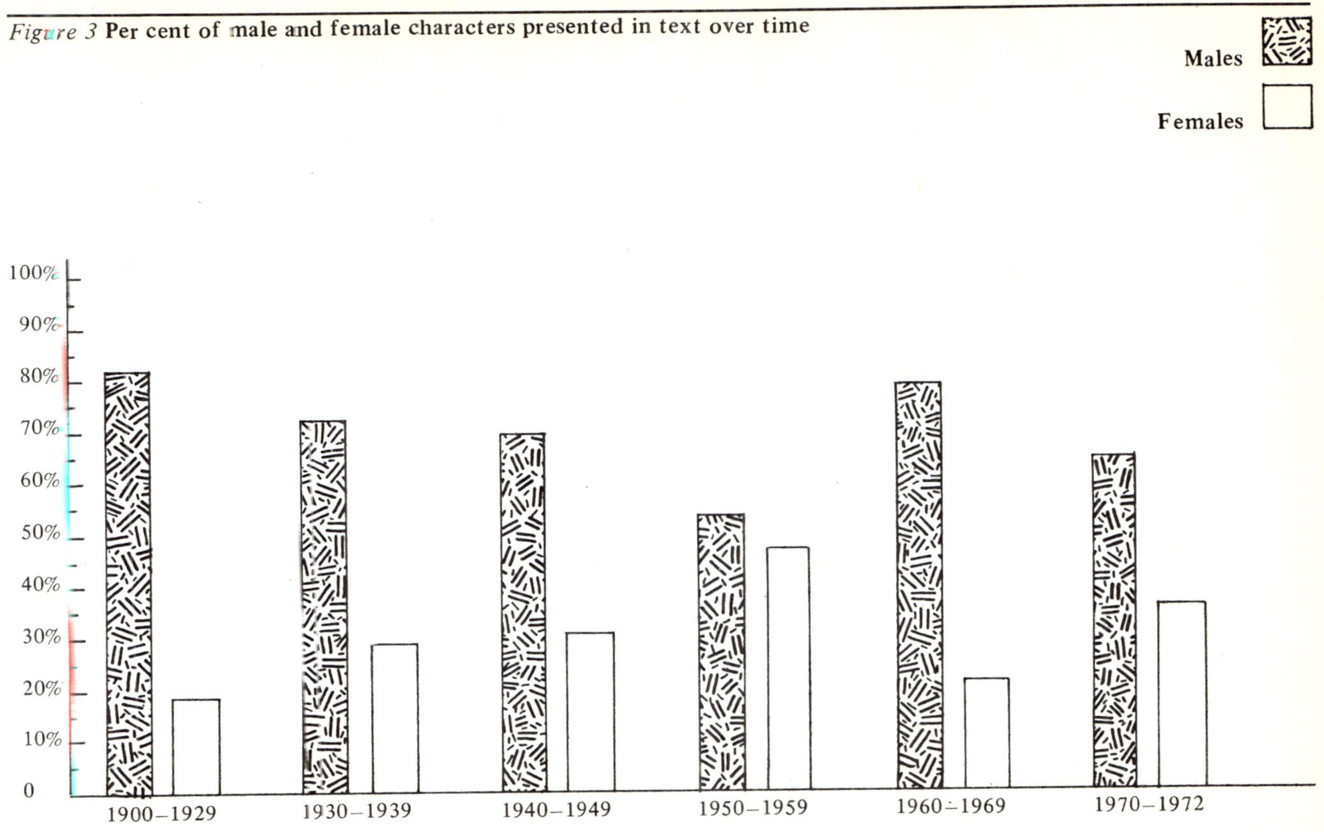

Sex-Roles in Reading Schemes

Glenys Lobban

The major premise underlying the current debate about class and race bias in reading schemes is that the content of the schemes influences children's attitudes to the world and to themselves. Reading schemes are presumed to be particularly influential because they are usually the child's first introduction to the written word and they are presented within a context of authority, the classroom, and most children read them. They are hence presumed to convey official approval of attitudes the child will have already learned in the pre-school years from parents, the media and other persons in the society. Current knowledge suggests that children's books and particularly their first readers do influence children's attitudes. They do this by presenting models like themselves for the children to identify with and emulate. In addition they present an official view of the real world and 'proper' attitudes.

It is now generally agreed that reading schemes such as the *Ladybird* scheme, which show a white middle-class world peopled with daddies in suits, and mummies in frilly aprons, who take tea on the lawns in front of their detached houses, are likely to be irrelevant and harmful for urban working-class and black children. They do not provide them with models like themselves, they implicitly, if not explicitly, denigrate these children's culture and imply that what is real and proper is also white and middle-class. If this argument is accepted for race and class bias in reading schemes then it must equally apply to another type of inequality within our society, namely sexual inequality.

Ours is a patriarchal society where females are economically and legally discriminated against, where males control all the major social institutions, and where two distinct sex-roles, the 'feminine'-passive and the 'masculine'-active, exist. As nobody has proved any genetic difference between females

This article first appeared in *Forum − for the discussion of new trends in education* Spring 1974, Vol 16, no.2. Reprinted by kind permission of the author and editor.

and males other than those related to reproduction, we must conclude that the sex differences in temperament, interests, abilities and goals, are the results of socialisation. If we assume that despite class and race discrimination in our society, reading schemes should not mirror this and denigrate these groups, then we should also demand that such schemes do not mirror male-dominated sex-roles and denigrate females.

To my knowledge few people have extended the argument in this way, and indeed no broad-ranging study of the way sex-roles are presented in British reading schemes even exists. This article will describe a preliminary study on sex-role content in readers which I undertook to begin to remedy this lack of information.

The sex-role content of six popular British reading schemes was coded. I chose two schemes published before 1960 (*Janet and John* and *Happy Venture*), two published in the 60s (*Ready to Read* and *Ladybird*), and two recent schemes (*Nipper* and *Breakthrough to Literacy*) which are designed specifically for urban children. I coded the content of 225 stories in all. 179 of these had people as their central characters and I listed the toys and pets, activities and adult roles these showed for each sex and both the sexes. Table 1 gives a summary of these results. It lists the toys and pets, activities and adult roles for each and both of the sexes that figured in three or more of the six reading schemes. In all cases single sex activities are those which figured as single sex in five of the schemes and in some of the readers in the remaining scheme.

A glance at Table 1 shows that the schemes rigidly divided the sphere of people's activity into two compartments, 'masculine' and 'feminine' with very few common characteristics. The number of 'masculine' options exceeded the number of 'feminine' ones in every category and they tended to be more active and instrumental and to relate more to the outside world and the outdoors than the 'feminine' options which revolved almost entirely around domestic roles. Only 35 of the 179 stories I coded had heroines, while 71 had heroes. The heroines were seldom being successful in non-'feminine' spheres, while the heroes were frequently brave and adventurous. In the *Nipper* scheme, for example, a heroine who ran away got lost, caught the wrong tube and found herself back home and gave up, whereas boys who went off on their own frequently found adventure. In the remaining 73 stories there were female and male central characters but it was almost always a boy who took the lead in all non domestic activities and let the girl help or watch. In the *Janet and John* scheme, for example, while both children had dogs, Janet's was a puppy while John had a big dog. Boys were more frequently responsible for the care of the pets, and owned larger versions of a common toy such as a boat, and usually did better at common activities; eg, the boy reached the top of the tree while sister sat on a lower branch. In the classroom situation both sexes were equally good at reading and writing, but they were frequently shown with toys or apparatus conventionally appropriate to their sex. Frequently in situations where the

39

Table 1 The sex-roles that occurred in three or more of the six schemes coded

THE SEX FOR WHICH THE ROLE WAS PRESCRIBED	THE CONTENT OF THE CHILDREN'S ROLES					THE ADULT ROLES PRESENTED
	TOYS AND PETS	ACTIVITIES	TAKING THE LEAD IN BOTH SEX ACTIVITIES	LEARNING A NEW SKILL	
GIRLS ONLY	1. Doll 2. Skipping rope 3. Doll's pram	1. Preparing the tea 2. Playing with dolls 3. Taking care of younger siblings	1. Hopping 2. Shopping with parents 3. Skipping	1. Taking care of younger siblings	1. Mother 2. Aunt 3. Grandmother
BOYS ONLY	1. Car 2. Train 3. Aeroplane 4. Boat 5. Football	1. Playing with cars 2. Playing with trains 3. Playing football 4. Lifting or pulling heavy objects 5. Playing cricket 6. Watching adult males in occupational roles 7. Heavy gardening	1. Going exploring alone 2. Climbing trees 3. Building things 4. Taking care of pets 5. Sailing boats 6. Flying kites 7. Washing and polishing Dad's car	1. Taking care of pets 2. Making/Building 3. Saving/Rescuing people or pets 4. Playing sports	1. Father 2. Uncle 3. Grandfather 4. Postman 5. Farmer 6. Fisherman 7. Shop or business owner 8. Policeman 9. Builder 10. Bus driver 11. Bus conductor 12. Train driver 13. Railway porter
BOTH SEXES	1. Book 2. Ball 3. Paints 4. Bucket and spade 5. Dog 6. Cat 7. Shop	1. Playing with pets 2. Writing 3. Reading 4. Going to the seaside 5. Going on a family outing	—	—	1. Teacher 2. Shop assistant

children participated equally, their parents played out conventional roles. When both sexes made or built anything the boy usually did so more or excelled and Dad was the instructor unless they were learning to make cakes. Mum was never shown teaching them to build anything or to play sport.

It is illuminating to contrast the female and male worlds the schemes showed. The female world was almost entirely oriented around domestic activity and childcare. The message that the schemes conveyed was that a woman's place is in the home and that little girls should spend their time learning 'feminine' skills such as cooking and childcare. It is significant that the only new skill learned by girls in three or more of the schemes was taking care of a younger sibling. The adult models available were all situated in the home and shown doing domestic activity. The *Nipper* scheme was the only one which showed working mothers and this was for a minority of the mothers shown. The fact is that the majority of women in Britain are in paid employment outside the home and many of them are neither shop assistants nor teachers (the only both sex jobs in the schemes). This makes the schemes' relegation of women to the home even more invidious. The only two girls' activities that allowed physical activity were skipping and hopping. Neither of these develop group co-operation nor the varied motor skills that the range of boys' activities and games offered.

The male world the schemes described did not include toys or activities that allowed expressive or nurturant behaviour. Boys' toys and activities were such as to allow the learning of independence and a variety of instrumental and motor skills. The boys' world was oriented outside the home and their toys and their adult models suggested a variety of future occupational

A typical example of sexism in British reading schemes.

goals. Boys, unlike girls, spent time watching adult males, who weren't relatives, performing their occupational roles. The idea that it was the boys who would have jobs was often explicitly stated. While girls were told they'd be like Mum or voiced such ideas, the boys expressed the desire to be train-drivers and the like. In only one of the *Nipper* readers was a jobless father shown, and this dad was just temporarily out of work, while virtually all mums were jobless permanently. Thus, while the scope of adult male roles was somewhat limited, the schemes clearly conveyed the idea that it was males who had jobs, and who were responsible for the maintenance of all aspects of the 'real' world except for childcare and cooking.

The schemes also showed the interaction within the family in rigidly traditional terms. *Nipper* was the only scheme which showed female single parent families and none of the schemes showed male single parent units. None of the schemes showed Dad doing housework or cooking anything other than a cup of tea. (The one exception was in *Ready to Read* when Mum was in hospital having a baby.) Dad was always the one who drove 'his' car (only one reader in one scheme showed a woman driver), his authority was ultimate and he usually initiated and directed all family activities. All the schemes abounded in pictures of Dad reading the paper or watching television, while Mum bustled about preparing and serving food, and washing up, often with the help of daughter. Once again, as in the case of female employment, the schemes' version of the family was even more rigidly traditional than current practice. Many British women drive cars and do handiwork, and in many homes cooking and cleaning are tasks which are shared by the family, but none of this was reflected in the schemes.

In summary the reading schemes showed a 'real' world peopled by women and girls who were almost solely involved with domestic activity and whom the adventurous and innovative males might occasionally allow into their world (the rest of human activity and achievement) in a helpmate capacity. The world they depicted was not only sexist, it was more sexist than present reality, and in many ways totally foreign to the majority of children, who do have working Mums, and at least some experience of cross sex activities.

The question that now arises concerns the impact of these readers on the attitudes of girls and boys to themselves and the world. If, as research suggests, characters like themselves suggest new modes of behaviour for children and define what they should do and want, then the models of their own sex available to the readers could only serve to reinforce the patriarchal sex-roles the children have already learned. The present policy in primary schools (see the Plowden Report) is for all the pupils to do traditionally one sex activities like cooking and metalwork. The content of the reading schemes is opposite to this policy, and might well neutralise these non-sextyped experiences, or convince the children that experiences in school are unrelated to the 'real' world outside. The schemes, like the rest of children's and adults' literature (see Millett, 1970), concentrate on the exploits of males. The girls who read them have already been schooled to

I hear her in the kitchen.

A typical example of sexism in British reading schemes.

believe, as our society does, that males are superior to females and better at everything other than domestic work, and the stories in the schemes cannot but reinforce the damage that our society does to girls' self-esteem. The total lack of female characters who are successful in non-'feminine' activities and jobs and who are independent, ensures that girls with these aspirations will receive no encouragement. In the same way, boys who feel the need to express gentleness and nurturance will find no male models to emulate. In short, these schemes in no way question the correctness of a society which deprives both sexes of full expression of their capabilities, and, in fact, they endorse a set of sex-roles that are even more rigid than our present role division.

One of the arguments that might be given to justify male bias in reading schemes is that boys have more reading problems. Certainly girls learn to read in spite of the male bias in readers but at what price to their self attitudes? If the primers children were given paid them the compliment of being intelligent beings able to comprehend complexity and depicted a world real to the majority of children (with girls who were tough, children of varied colour and nationalities, boys who cried, motherless or fatherless families, working parents, family fights, violence, television and other phenomena familiar to them) they would involve all the children. If we as educationalists care about the full development of each individual child it is time we became fully aware of how materials such as reading schemes denigrate females as well as other groups. It is time we acknowledged and attempted to change this sexist aspect of their content, and of our society, along with the class and race inequalities.

References

1. **Reading Schemes used**
   a. **Breakthrough to Literacy.** D Mackay, B Thompson and P Schuaub. London: Longmans, for the Schools Council, 1970.
   b. **Happy Venture Reader.** F J Schonell and I Sarjeant. London: Oliver & Boyd, 1958.
   c. **Janet and John.** M O'Donnell and R Munro. Herts: James Nisbet & Co, 1950.
   d. **Ladybird Key Words Reading Scheme.** W Murray. Loughborough: Wills & Hepworth Ltd, 1964.
   e. **Nipper.** London: Macmillan Ltd, 1968.
   f. **Ready to Read.** M Simpson. London: Methuen, 1964.

2. **References cited in text**
   a. Millett, K. **Sexual Politics.** New York: Doubleday & Co Inc, 1970.
   b. Plowden Report. **Children and their Primary Schools.** London: HMSO, 1963.

The McGraw-Hill Guidelines

Guidelines for equal treatment of the sexes

Introduction

The word *sexism* was coined, by analogy to *racism*, to denote discrimination based on gender. In its original sense, *sexism* referred to prejudice against the female sex. In a broader sense, the term now indicates any arbitrary stereotyping of males and females on the basis of their gender.

We are endeavouring through these guidelines to eliminate sexist assumptions from McGraw-Hill Book Company publications and to encourage a greater freedom for all individuals to pursue their interests and realize their potentials. Specifically, these guidelines are designed to make McGraw-Hill staff members and McGraw-Hill authors aware of the ways in which males and females have been stereotyped in publications; to show the role language has played in reinforcing inequality; and to indicate positive approaches toward providing fair, accurate, and balanced treatment of both sexes in our publications.

One approach is to recruit more women as authors and contributors in all fields. The writings and viewpoints of women should be represented in quotations and references whenever possible. Anthologies should include a larger proportion of selections by and about women in fields where suitable materials are available but women are currently under-represented.

Women as well as men have been leaders and heroes, explorers and pioneers, and have made notable contributions to science, medicine, law, business, politics, civics, economics, literature, the arts, sports, and other areas of endeavour. Books dealing with subjects like these, as well as general histories, should acknowledge the achievements of women. The fact that women's rights, opportunities, and accomplishments have been limited by the social customs and conditions of their time should be openly discussed whenever relevant to the topic at hand.

We realize that the language of literature cannot be prescribed. The recommendations in these guidelines, thus, are intended primarily for use in teaching materials, reference works, and nonfiction works in general.

McGraw-Hill Book Company, USA, issued these Guidelines for the benefit of their editorial staff and authors on 27.5.74.

Non-Sexist Treatment of Women and Men
Men and women should be treated primarily as people, and not primarily as members of opposite sexes. Their shared humanity and common attributes should be stressed — not their gender difference. Neither sex should be stereotyped or arbitrarily assigned to a leading or secondary role.

Avoid Masculine and Feminine Stereotypes
• Though many women will continue to choose traditional occupations such as homemaker or secretary, women should not be type-cast in these roles but shown in a wide variety of professions and trades: as doctors and dentists, not always as nurses; as principals and professors, not always as teachers; as lawyers and judges, not always as social workers; as bank presidents, not always as tellers; as members of Congress, not always as members of the League of Women Voters.
• Similarly, men should not be shown as constantly subject to the "masculine mystique" in their interests, attitudes, or careers. They should not be made to feel that their self-worth depends entirely upon their income level or the status level of their jobs. They should not be conditioned to believe that a man ought to earn more than a woman or that he ought to be the sole support of a family.
• An attempt should be made to break job stereotypes for both women and men. No job should be considered sex-typed, and it should never be implied that certain jobs are incompatible with a woman's "femininity" or a man's "masculinity." Thus, women as well as men should be shown as accountants, engineers, pilots, plumbers, bridge-builders, computer operators, TV repairers, and astronauts, while men as well as women should be shown as nurses, grade-school teachers, secretaries, typists, librarians, file clerks, switchboard operators, and baby-sitters.

Women within a profession should be shown at all professional levels, including the top levels. Women should be portrayed in positions of authority over men and over other women, and there should be no implication that a man loses face or that a woman faces difficulty if the employer or supervisor is a woman. All work should be treated as honorable and worthy of respect; no job or job choices should be downgraded. Instead, women and men should be offered more options than were available to them when work was stereotyped by sex.
• Books designed for children at the pre-school, elementary, and secondary levels should show married women who work outside the home and should treat them favorably. Teaching materials should not assume or imply that most women are wives who are also full-time mothers, but should instead emphasize the fact that women have choices about their marital status, just

as men do: that some women choose to stay permanently single and some are in no hurry to marry; that some women marry but do not have children, while others marry, have children, and continue to work outside the home. Thus, a text might say that some married people have children and some do not, and that sometimes *one or both parents* work outside the home. Instructional materials should never imply that all women have a "mother instinct" or that the emotional life of a family suffers because a woman works. Instead they might state that when both parents work outside the home there is usually either greater sharing of the child-rearing activities or reliance on day-care centers, nursery schools, or other help.

According to Labor Department statistics for 1972, over 42 per cent of all mothers with children under 18 worked outside the home, and about a third of these working mothers had children under 6. Publications ought to reflect this reality.

Both men and women should be shown engaged in home maintenance activities, ranging from cooking and housecleaning to washing the car and making household repairs. Sometimes the man should be shown preparing the meals, doing the laundry, or diapering the baby, while the woman builds bookcases or takes out the trash.

• Girls should be shown as having, and exercising, the same options as boys in their play and career choices. In school materials, girls should be encouraged to show an interest in mathematics, mechanical skills, and active sports, for example, while boys should never be made to feel ashamed of an interest in poetry, art, or music, or an aptitude for cooking, sewing, or child care. Course materials should be addressed to students of both sexes. For example, home economics courses should apply to boys as well as girls, and shop to girls as well as boys. Both males and females should be shown in textbook illustrations depicting career choices.

When as a practical matter it is known that a book will be used primarily by women for the life of the edition (say, the next five years), it is pointless to pretend that the readership is divided equally between males and females. In such cases it may be more beneficial to address the book fully to women and exploit every opportunity (1) to point out to them a broader set of options than they might otherwise have considered, and (2) to encourage them to aspire to a more active, assertive, and policymaking role than they might otherwise have thought of.

Women and girls should be portrayed as active participants in the same proportion as men and boys in stories, examples, problems, illustrations, discussion questions, test items, and exercises, regardless of subject matter. Women should not be stereotyped in examples by being spoken of only in connection with cooking, sewing, shopping and similar activities.

Emphasize Common Human Characteristics
• Members of both sexes should be represented as whole human beings with *human* strengths and weaknesses, not masculine or feminine ones. Women and girls should be shown as having the same abilities, interests, and ambitions as men and boys. Characteristics that have been traditionally praised in males — such as boldness, initiative, and assertiveness — should also be praised in females. Characteristics that have been praised in females — such as gentleness, compassion, and sensitivity — should also be praised in males.
• Like men and boys, women and girls should be portrayed as independent, active, strong, courageous, competent, decisive, persistent, serious-minded, and successful. They should appear as logical thinkers, problem-solvers, and decision makers. They should be shown as interested in their work, pursuing a variety of career goals, and both deserving of and receiving public recognition for their accomplishments.
• Sometimes men should be shown as quiet and passive, or fearful and indecisive, or illogical and immature. Similarly, women should sometimes be shown as tough, aggressive, and insensitive. Stereotypes of the logical, objective male and the emotional, subjective female are to be avoided. In descriptions, the smarter, braver, or more successful person should be a woman or girl as often as a man or boy. In illustrations, the taller, heavier, stronger, or more active person should not always be male, especially when children are portrayed.

Equality in Description will mean an end to the Sexual Cliche
• Women and men should be treated with the same respect, dignity, and seriousness. Neither should be trivialized or stereotyped, either in text or in illustrations. Women should not be described by physical attributes when men are being described by mental attributes or professional position. Instead, both sexes should be dealt with in the same terms. References to a man's or a woman's appearance, charm, or intuition should be avoided when irrelevant.

NO	YES
Henry Harris is a shrewd lawyer and his wife Ann is a striking brunette.	The Harrises are an attractive couple. Henry is a handsome blond and Ann is a striking brunette.
	The Harrises are highly respected in their fields. Ann is an accomplished

musician and Henry is a shrewd lawyer.

The Harrises are an interesting couple. Henry is a shrewd lawyer and Ann is very active in community (*or* church *or* civic) affairs.

- In descriptions of women, a patronizing or girl-watching tone should be avoided, as should sexual innuendoes, jokes, and puns. Examples of practices to be avoided: focusing on physical appearance (a buxom blonde); using special female-gender word forms (*poetess, aviatrix, usherette*); treating women as sex objects or portraying the typical woman as weak, helpless, or hysterical; making women figures of fun or objects of scorn and treating their issues as humorous or unimportant.

Examples of stereotypes to be avoided: scatter-brained female, fragile flower, goddess on a pedestal, catty gossip, henpecking shrew, apron-wearing mother, frustrated spinster, ladylike little girl. Jokes at women's expense — such as the woman driver or nagging mother-in-law cliches — are to be avoided.

NO	YES
the fair sex; the weaker sex	*women*
the distaff side	*the female side or line*
the girls or *the ladies* (when adult females are meant)	*the women*
girl, as in: I'll have my *girl* check that.	I'll have my *secretary* (or my *assistant*) check that. (Or use the person's name.)
lady used as a modifier, as in *lady lawyer.*	*lawyer* (A woman may be identified simply through the choice of pronouns, as in: *The lawyer made her summation to the jury.* Try to avoid gender modifiers altogether. When you *must* modify, use *woman* or *female,* as in: *a course on women writers,* or *the airline's first female pilot.*)

49

the little woman; the better half; the ball and chain	wife
female-gender word forms, such as *authoress, poetess, Jewess*	*author, poet, Jew*
female-gender or diminutive word forms, such as *suffragette, usherette, aviatrix*	*suffragist, usher, aviator* (or pilot)
libber (a put-down)	*feminist; liberationist*
sweet young thing	*young woman; girl*
co-ed (as a noun)	student

(*Note:* Logically, *co-ed* should refer to any student at a co-educational college or university. Since it does not, it is a sexist term.)

housewife	*homemaker* for a person who works at home, or rephrase with a more precise or more inclusive term.
The sound of the drilling disturbed the housewives in the neighbourhood.	The sound of the drilling disturbed everyone within earshot (or everyone in the neighbourhood).
Housewives are feeling the pinch of higher prices.	Consumers (customers or shoppers) are feeling the pinch of higher prices.
career girl or career woman	name the woman's profession: *attorney Ellen Smith; Maria Sanchez, a journalist* or editor or business executive or doctor or lawyer or agent.
cleaning woman, cleaning lady, or *maid*	*housekeeper; house* or *office cleaner*

• In descriptions of men, especially men in the home, references to general ineptness should be avoided. Men should not be characterized as dependent on women for meals, or clumsy in household maintenance, or as foolish in self-care.

To be avoided: characterizations that stress men's dependence on women for advice on what to wear and what to eat, inability of men to care for themselves in times of illness, and men as objects of fun (the henpecked husband).

• Women should be treated as part of the rule, not as the exception.

Generic terms, such as doctor and nurse, should be assumed to include both men and women, and modified titles such as "woman doctor" or "male nurse" should be avoided. Work should never be stereotyped as "woman's work" or as "a man-sized job". Writers should avoid showing a "gee-whiz" attitude toward women who perform competently; ("Though a woman, she ran the business as well as any man" or "Though a woman, she ran the business efficiently").

• Women should be spoken of as participants in the action, not as possessions of the men. Terms such as *pioneer, farmer,* and *settler* should not be used as though they applied only to adult males.

NO	YES
Pioneers moved West, taking their wives and children with them.	Pioneer families moved West.
	Pioneer men and women (*or* pioneer couples) moved West, taking their children with them.

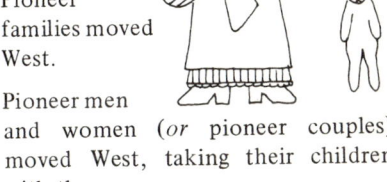

• Women should not be portrayed as needing male permission in order to act or to exercise rights (except, of course, for historical or factual accuracy).

NO	YES
Jim Weiss allows his wife to work part-time.	Judy Weiss works part-time.

Recognition and Respect
Women should be recognized for their own achievements. Intelligent, daring, and innovative women, both in history and in fiction, should be provided as role-models for girls, and leaders in the fight for women's rights should be honoured and respected, not mocked or ignored.

The Problems of Rewording
In references to humanity at large, language should operate to include women and girls. Terms that tend to exclude females should be avoided whenever possible.

• The word *man* has long been used not only to denote a person of male gender, but also generically to denote humanity at large. To many people today, however, the word *man* has become so closely associated with the first meaning (a male human being) that they consider it no longer broad enough to be applied to any person or to human beings as a whole. In deference to this position, alternative expressions should be used in place of *man* (or derivative constructions used generically to signify humanity at large) whenever such substitutions can be made without producing an awkward or artificial construction. In cases where *man*-words must be used, special efforts should be made to ensure that pictures and other devices make explicit that

51

such references include women.

Here are some possible substitutions for *man*-words:

NO	YES
mankind	humanity, human beings, human race, people
primitive man	primitive people or peoples; primitive human beings; primitive men and women
man's achievements	human achievements
If a man drove 50 miles at 60mph ...	If a person (or driver) drove 50 miles at 60mph ...
the best man for the job	the best person (or candidate) for the job
manmade	artificial; synthetic, manufactured; constructed; of human origin
manpower	human power; human energy; workers; workforce
grow to manhood	grow to adulthood; grow to manhood or womanhood

- The English language lacks a generic singular pronoun signifying *he* or *she*, and therefore it has been customary and grammatically sanctioned to use masculine pronouns in expressions such as "one ... *he*", "anyone ... *he*", and "each child opens *his* book". Nevertheless, avoid when possible the pronouns *he, him,* and *his* in reference to the hypothetical person or humanity in general.

Various alternatives may be considered:
1 Reword to eliminate unnecessary gender pronouns.

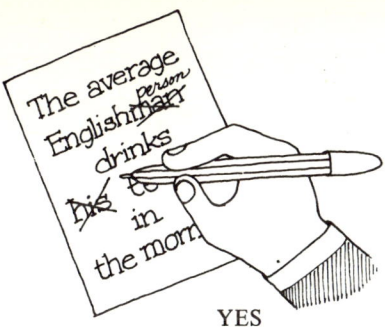

NO
The average American drinks his coffee black.

YES
The average American drinks black coffee.

2 Recast into the plural

Most Americans drink their coffee black.

3 Replace the masculine pronoun with *one, you, he or she, her or his,* as appropriate. (Use *he or she* and its variations sparingly to avoid clumsy prose.)

4 Alternate male and female expressions and examples.

NO
I've often heard supervisors say, "He's not the right man for the job", or "He lacks the qualifications for success."

YES
I've often heard supervisors say, "She's not the right person for the job", or "He lacks the qualifications for success."

5 To avoid severe problems of repetition or inept wording, it may sometimes be best to use the generic term *he* freely, but to add, in the preface and as often as necessary in the text, emphatic statements to the effect that the masculine pronouns are being used for succinctness and are intended to refer to both females and males.

These guidelines can only suggest a few solutions to difficult problems of rewording. The proper solution in any given passage must depend on the context and on the author's intention. For example, it would be wrong to pluralize in contexts stressing a one-to-one relationship, as between teacher and child. In such cases, either using the expression *he or she* or alternating *he* and *she*, as appropriate, will be acceptable.

• Occupational terms ending in *man* should be replaced whenever possible by terms that can include members of either sex unless they refer to a particular person.

NO
congressman

YES
member of Congress; representative (but Congress*man* Koch and Congress*woman* Holtzman)

businessman	business executive; business manager
fireman	fire fighter
mailman	mail carrier; letter carrier
salesman	sales representative; sales-person; sales clerk
insurance man	insurance agent
statesman	leader; public servant
chairman	the person presiding at (or chairing) a meeting; the presiding officer; the chair; head; leader; coordinator; moderator
cameraman	camera operator
foreman	supervisor

- Language that assumes all readers are male should be avoided.

NO	YES
you and your wife	you and your spouse
when you shave in the morning	when you brush your teeth (or wash up) in the morning

Non-Sexist and Equal use of Language
The language used to designate and describe females and males should treat the sexes equally.
- Parallel language should be used for women and men.

NO	YES
the men and the ladies	the men and the women; the ladies and the gentlemen; the girls and the boys

man and wife   husband and wife

Note that *lady* and *gentleman, wife* and *husband,* and *mother* and *father* are role words. *Ladies* should be used for women only when men are being referred to as *gentlemen.* Similarly, women should be called *wives* and *mothers* only when men are referred to as *husbands* and *fathers.* Like a male shopper, a woman in a grocery store should be called a *customer,* not a *housewife.*
• Women should be identified by their own names (e.g., Indira Gandhi). They should not be referred to in terms of their roles as wife, mother, sister, or daughter unless it is in these roles that they are significant in context. Nor should they be identified in terms of their marital relationships (Mrs. Gandhi) unless this brief form is stylistically more convenient (than, say Prime Minister Gandhi) or is paired up with similar references to men.
1 A woman should be referred to by name in the same way that a man is. Both should be called by their full names, by first or last name only, or by title.

NO
Bobby Riggs and Billie Jean

Billie Jean and Riggs; Mrs. King and Riggs

Mrs. Meir and Moshe Dayan

YES
Bobby Riggs and Billie Jean King

Billie Jean and Bobby; King and Riggs; Ms. King (because she prefers Ms.) and Mr. Riggs

Golda Meir and Moshe Dayan, or Mrs. Meir and Mr. Dayan

2 Unnecessary reference to or emphasis on a woman's marital status should be avoided. Whether married or not, a woman may be referred to by the name by which she chooses to be known, whether her name is her original name or her married name.
• Whenever possible a term should be used that includes both sexes. Unnecessary references to gender should be avoided.

NO
college boys and co-eds

YES
students

• Insofar as possible, job titles should be non-sexist. Different nomenclature should not be used for the same job depending on whether it is held by a male or by a female. (See also above for additional examples of words ending in *man*.)

NO	YES
steward or purser or stewardess	flight attendant
policeman and policewoman	police officer
maid and houseboy	house or office cleaner; servant

• Different pronouns should not be linked with certain work or occupations on the assumption that the worker is always (or usually) female or male. Instead, either pluralize or use *he or she* and *she or he*.

NO	YES
the consumer or shopper . . . she	consumers or shoppers . . . they
the secretary . . . she	secretaries . . . they
the breadwinner . . . his earnings	the breadwinner . . . his or her earnings *or* breadwinners . . . their earnings.

• Males should not always be first in order of mention. Instead, alternate the order, sometimes using: *women and men, gentlemen and ladies, she or he, her or his.*

Conclusion

It is hoped that these guidelines have alerted authors and staff members to the problems of sex discrimination and to various ways of solving them.

56

ELENA GIANINI BELOTTI

LITTLE GIRLS

"This book, from Italy, takes us even further than most in showing us how stereotyping pressures act on us all our lives..." Times Educational Supplement

"... It takes the iron hand in the velvet glove, not just in the already familiar trains-for-boys dolls-for-girls domestic-science carpentry syndrome but way back to pre-natal influences." Jill Tweedie, The Guardian

"A most helpful and thought-provoking addition to the literature in the area of sexual discrimination..." International Playground Association Newsletter

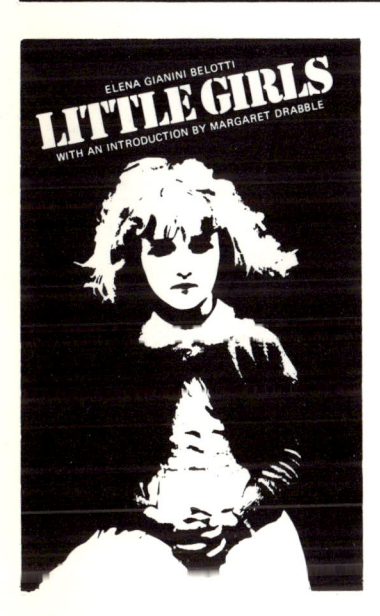

This internationally-acclaimed book vividly describes the ways in which children, from earliest infancy onwards, are forced into sexually-delineated roles. With tact and insight, Belotti investigates the ways in which parental attitudes, widely-held cultural assumptions, schooling, as well as children's games, toys and literature all conspire to mould little boys — irrespective of their individual attributes — into active, aggressive men, and more specifically, little girls into submissive housewives and mothers. Belotti's analysis of children's literature has sparked a new series of non-sexist books for children. 85p

◉ Writers and Readers Publishing Cooperative

Non-sexist Children's Literature

Before the turtle Arthur marries Clementine, she thinks that life together will be a great adventure. But it's not. Arthur constantly derides her when she wants to be creative and simply brings her more and more possessions, thinking that these will satisfy her. Eventually Clementine decides to leave him and all his burdensome presents and goes off to roam the world, making music as she goes.

The Bonobos are male monkeys whose 'culture' consists of an ability to scream out four newly learned French words. For this they get a diploma — a pair of sunglasses. But their wives, the Bonobosses can do this too, and *their* ability goes unrewarded. So, they leave with their Bonobabies to found a new and peaceful society. Who knows if the Bonobos ever rejoined them? It all happened a very long time ago.

Our new series of Non-Sexist Children's Literature sets out to provide children with patterns of behaviour which break away from conventional models.

These four titles are the first in the series, providing children with some alternatives to the kind of books available at the moment, which portray a world dominated by men and male values.

In these new books, women and girls defy the restrictions conventionally placed on them.

At a time when women everywhere are redefining their roles and engaging more fully in all sectors of life, children's books which reflect this change and champion it are essential.

The stories are written by Adela Turin and illustrated by Nella Bosnia.

These four books, which are casebound and beautifully illustrated in full colour cost £2.50 each.

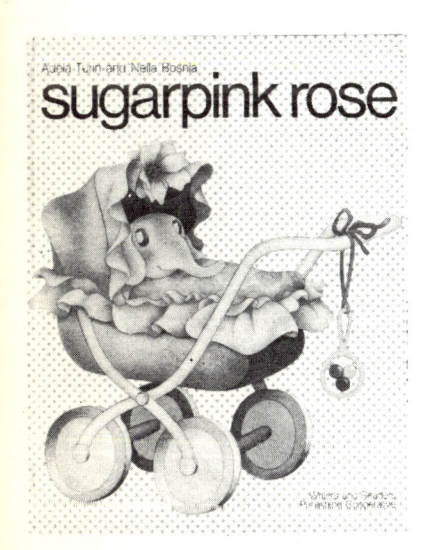

The elephant Annabelle is sick of eating anemones and peonies which make little girl elephants turn sugarpink rose in colour. She rebels, refuses to turn pink and leaves the flower enclosure to play in streams and savannas. Seeing how much fun Annabelle's life has become, all the other little girl elephants join her until only grey elephants are to be seen in elephant land.

Before the flood, the retelling of Father Ratigan's heroic exploits was all the excitement that Mother Ratigan and her family had from life; but because of the flood, Mother Ratigan's resourcefulness and real abilities are revealed and she and her children learn to create their own amusements.

Writers and Readers Publishing Cooperative

Racist and Sexist Images in Children's Books
Council on Interracial Books for Children 35p

The anti-racist articles in this pamphlet provide a starting point for debate and for developing fresh challenges to racist attitudes. Various well-known children's books, including **Charlie and the Chocolate Factory, Sounder** and **Dr. Dolittle** receive criticism for their images of Black people and Black experience. Sexism is as fundamental an issue as racism to be attacked: the description of children's books from China provides a positive example of the fight against sex-stereotyping. This was the first of our **Papers on Children's Literature** in which we are attempting to publish material which will analyse the stereotypes, omissions and distortions too commonly found in children's books.

BULLETIN

The articles in Racist and Sexist Images in Children's Books first appeared in the **Bulletin** of the U.S. based Council on Interracial Books for Children. The **Bulletin** regularly evaluates children's materials — trade books (both new and classics), textbooks, reading programmes and other educational materials — for their messages about racism, sexism and classism. Articles focus on such related topics as library school curriculums, pre-school and nursery programmes, career education, etc. Resource groups, alternative materials and suggestions for combatting stereotypes, distortions and omissions are given.

Subscribe today. Annual rates are (8 issues):
£4 for individuals £2.50 for students £7.25 for libraries, schools.

Above rates are for surface mail. Please add £2.50 for airmail. Please make cheques payable to CIBC and send orders to:
The Bulletin, CIBC, 1841 Broadway, New York NY 10023, USA